Fiction Sequels
for Readers 10 to 16

Fiction Sequels for Readers 10 to 16

An Annotated Bibliography of Books in Succession

VICKI ANDERSON

McFarland & Company, Inc., Publishers
Jefferson, North Carolina, and London

British Library Cataloguing-in-Publication data are available

Library of Congress Cataloguing-in-Publication Data

Anderson, Vicki, 1928–
    Fiction sequels for readers 10 to 16 : an annotated bibliography
of books in succession / Vicki Anderson.
        p.   cm.
    [Includes index.]
    Summary: Provides annotations for approximately 1500 sequel books.
    ISBN 0-89950-519-8 (sewn softcover : 50# alk. paper) ⊖
    1. Children's stories—Bibliography.   2. Young adult fiction—
Bibliography.   3. Sequels (Literature)—Bibliography.
    [1. Fiction—Bibliography.   2. Sequels (Literature)—Bibliography.]
    I. Title.
    Z1037.A53   1990
    [PN1009.A1]
    016.80883—dc20   89-43686
                                                               CIP
                                                                AC

Manufactured in the United States of America

McFarland & Company, Inc., Publishers
  Box 611, Jefferson, North Carolina 28640

Many thanks to
the San Diego Public Library
and the San Diego City Schools

Table of Contents

Introduction

The last 25 years has seen an astonishing growth in sequel (or succession) books.

As I worked as a librarian over the years it occurred to me that I needed a complete list of these books for several reasons—to answer requests for "another one like this one"; to keep my collection of them annotated; to assure that I purchased needed volumes; to make reader's guidance programs more flexible, and so on.

When working with readers it is important to do a follow-up when they come back asking for "another one like it." If it is a sequel and you know it, your job is made easier. When introducing a book, knowing it has a follow-up can help "sell" it.

We've all had the experience of suddenly finding ourselves with book one or book three of a trilogy and having never bought book two. We've also found ourselves trying to help a patron select a good book not knowing that it was part of a trilogy and so offer book three before book one. So in these situations and in any reader's guidance service, knowing instantly what is a sequel or where in a sequence a particular title belongs is important.

There is really no simple way to identify sequel books. The review journals do not always identify them as such. The catalog cards do not always do so. Even the book jacket, which is usually read after purchase, frequently doesn't.

The present book offers a key to these considerations; it deals with a wide range of sequels. It is intended to help librarians and readers sort out the sequels in any book collection.

The selection was as broad as I could make it. Since selectivity is never completely objective anyway, I chose to include almost all I could find. Therefore appropriateness, type and availability, and not the quality of writing, were used as a criteria.

The contents include books with literary value, as well as ones with easy readability, or that are high in popularity, or which attract the reluctant reader. There are many, of course, that challenge the true reader.

1

This book has a broad coverage. It includes stories about ethnic groups, families, sports, humor, etc. In other words you should find the proverbial well-rounded collection within these sequels, just as you'd find in your collection overall.

The titles selected are nearly all hardback books and have an interest level appropriate to children over 10. I have not put a great deal of emphasis on age group levels since experience has taught me that all readers are individuals and as such are not necessarily ready for the same book at the same time. Each child's tastes in books, current interests, social maturity and reading ability are different from those of other readers of the same age.

In her book *Sequences: An Annotated Guide to Children's Fiction in Series* Susan Roman states: "*Series* of fiction may or may not show an elaboration of character and plot through the individual titles. Within series there are stories that are more closely related to one another. These are *sequences*. Sequences do show this development of character and plot through each novel in the series. A *sequel* is a series title with the same characters as those in an earlier book. Often they may have only superficial unity."

In this collection a sequel is a book that can stand alone and be read and enjoyed by itself, but it is also a part of several books written about the same characters following a similar theme. Sometimes it is developmental and sometimes not. The books selected can be said simply to have a common thread reappearing in each book. Sometimes the character is the main character in all the books; sometimes a minor character in one book becomes a major character in another and vice versa. Sometimes they cover different members of the same family or different generations of the same family. Sometimes the character grows and matures through the books and sometimes they remain the same throughout all the books. These books are considered sequels because they have the same character in each book and continue the theme of an earlier work. This book is not about series or sequences but it is about sequels.

This list contains about 1500 titles by about 350 authors. As in most any list of books there are titles both included and excluded that users of this book may wonder about. I repeat: I included all I could find within the age group and time frame established. I'm sure there are more.

Some of the books listed herein may be out of print but since out-of-print books are still to be found on library shelves, or can be obtained on interlibrary loans, I didn't consider that important and have included them because of their value or interest and because readers should not miss them.

This list is not intended solely as a selection guide. It can be used to put identifying labels on the spines of the books indicating that it is part of a sequel and what part it is. (These labels can be purchased through any library supply house or can be made on site by using Avery labels.) In this way both librarian and readers would know which books are part of a larger group and which of them comes first.

It can be used to check the collection and see if it contains all volumes of the set.

It can be used as a promotional device to introduce sequel books to your readers. We know that if a reader comes back for book two or three we probably have captured another reader.

The arrangement is by author, listing the titles as they should be read (remember all these books can stand alone even though they are part of a sequel).

The annotations were gleaned from the books themselves, the book jackets, the catalog cards, the review journals and any other source I could find.

Publication date does not necessarily lead to the order of the sequels. Publication dates are included for bibliographic information only. There are several instances of *prequels,* that is, books written after the series was completed but giving background or earlier information about characters or situations in the series. These are enumerated with a "Pr."

I've listed no specific edition for well-known classics since there are so many available. It would depend on the needs of your library and the tastes of your readers. Otherwise brief bibliographic information is given. The publishers are given in short form—e.g., "Harper" for Harper and Row Publishing Company. The full names and addresses are easily available in many other publications, such as *Books in Print* and *Children's Catalog.*

The beginning date used for the original selection was 1960 but if some of the books in the series were written prior to 1960 they were included, as were those books I could determine were still being checked out by readers regardless of publication date. When some books have proved their stayability, especially in a sequel, it is best to keep them and all their companions on the shelves as long as readers are reading them.

There is a title index, showing in parentheses author last name and numerical position of the book in the sequence.

This book grew out of a need to know my collection better and to keep readers interested once they found a book they liked. My ultimate goal is to write the definitive "give me another one like it" bibliography. But that is some time off in the future and this is a first step. There are now in print several series lists, there is at least one list of sequences, and there are sequel lists for specific genres, all heading in this direction. Perhaps with this offering that day is nearer.

Vicki Anderson
December 1989

Fiction Sequels

Adler, Carole
1
Magic of the Glits
Macmillan, 1979
Glits are magical beings who can grant wishes. Jeremy and Lynette are kept entertained by "them" all summer.

Adler, Carole
2
Some Other Summer
Macmillan, 1982
Lynette, a 13-year-old orphan, is baffled and upset when her long-time friend, Jeremy, comes to spend the summer on her uncle's horse ranch and seems to ignore her.

Aiken, Joan
1
Wolves of Willoughby Chase
Doubleday, 1963
Bonnie and Sylvia escape from an orphanage where they are mistreated. Simon helps them in their many suspenseful, melodramatic misadventures.

Aiken, Joan
2
Black Hearts in Battersea
Doubleday, 1964
Simon, living homeless in London, stumbles upon a murder plan and has wild and exciting adventures on sea and in the air. His friend Dido has been lost at sea.

Aiken, Joan
3
Nightbirds on Nantucket
Doubleday, 1966
Dido is rescued at sea by an American ship but when she arrives at Nantucket her troubles begin again and she wants to return to England.

Aiken, Joan
4
Stolen Lake
Delacorte, 1981
Dido leaves Nantucket for London but her ship is detained at New Cumbria where she helps a queen, living in a revolving castle, recover her stolen lake!

Aiken, Joan
5
Cuckoo Tree
Doubleday, 1971
Dido, along with Captain Hughes, is again in England. An accident to the Captain gets Dido involved with King James IV's coronation.

Aiken, Joan
6
Dido and Pa
Delacorte, 1986
In this episode Dido Twite and Simon fight plotters against the King and her wicked father. Dido had been kidnapped by her father to use in his plan against the King.

Aiken, Joan
7
Whispering Mountain
Doubleday, 1969
Captain Hughes is afraid that his

grandson has stolen his magic harp, the Golden Harp of Teiter. But it is the strange beings living under Whispering Mountain who have it.

Aiken, Joan
A1
Arabel's Raven
Doubleday, 1974
Mortimer, the pet raven of Arabel, was injured when he was brought home by her father. He brings chaos wherever he goes. He cries "nevermore" when he is upset.

Aiken, Joan
A2
Arabel and Mortimer
Doubleday, 1981
Mortimer helps Arabel and her family when he is rewarded for finding a valuable ring. This helps offset all the minor nuisances he has caused since his arrival.

Aiken, Joan
A3
Mortimer's Cross
Harper, 1984
Mortimer gets involved with missing library books and a missing rock star. But, of course, he and Arabel solve them all.

Aiken, Joan
A4
Mortimer Says Nothing
Harper, 1985
This book contains four short stories about Mortimer and Arabel. They were all weird and hilarious.

Aiken, Joan
B1
Go Saddle the Sea
Doubleday, 1977
Felix runs away from the cold, loveless home of his grandfather in Spain and seeks to find some members of his father's family in England. He is both accused of murder and kidnapped.

Aiken, Joan
B2
Bridle the Wind
Doubleday, 1983
Felix, a 12-year-old orphan, sails back to Spain with an unexpected friend he has rescued from murder. The trip is not uneventful, including being shipwrecked.

Aiken, Joan
B3
Teeth of the Gale
Harper, 1988
Felix, now an 18-year-old, goes on a rescue journey across Spain at the request of a friendly nun. He and his friend Juana, run into spies and are attacked by bears as they search for a treasure.

Alcott, Louisa May
1
Little Women
1868
Meg, Jo, Beth and Amy are sisters in the March family. This is a story of their childhood experiences and the process of growing up in difficult times.

Alcott, Louisa May
2
Little Men
1871
The continuing March family saga: consisting of Jo and Meg's boys. Jo and her professor husband establish a school at Plumfield.

Alcott, Louisa May
3
Jo's Boys and How They Turned Out
1886
More stories about the March family. *Little Women* and the two sequels are well-known classics in literature for young readers.

Alcott, Louisa May
A1
Eight Cousins
1874
Rose, an orphan, lives with her aunt and Uncle Alec. She must learn to cope with their seven noisy sons, her cousins.

Alcott, Louisa May
A2

Rose in Bloom
1876

More about Rose as she grows up with many pleasures and a few disappointments. She meets a friend, Phoebe, and is being encouraged to marry one of her cousins with whom she has grown up.

Alexander, Lloyd
1
Westmark
Dutton, 1981

A young boy, fleeing from criminal charges, travels with Musket, Mickle and Count Las Bombas to a palace in Westmark where the king is in deep sorrow over his lost daughter.

Alexander, Lloyd
2
Kestrel
Dutton, 1982

Theo, Mickle and Muscrat are fighting bloody wars for the king and Westmark. Mickle takes her rightful place in the palace. Theo turns into an "animal" willing to kill but slowly recovers.

Alexander, Lloyd
3
Beggar Queen
Dutton, 1984

Mickle is now Queen Agusta and Theo is her consular. But peace doesn't last and Theo must fight again for Queen Agusta against Duke Conrad of Regia.

Alexander, Lloyd
PrA1
Foundling and Other Tales
Holt, 1973

Background tales about the times in Prydain before Taran was born.

Alexander, Lloyd
A1
Book of Three
Holt, 1964

Taran and Gwydion go off to fight the Horned King and his Cauldron Born. They are accompanied by many others whom we will meet in later books.

Alexander, Lloyd
A2
Black Cauldron
Holt, 1965

Taran fights the evil threat against Prydain and knows that to succeed he must destroy the Black Cauldron where living persons who sold themselves into evil are kept.

Alexander, Lloyd
A3
Castle of Llyr
Holt, 1966

Taran learns that he loves Eilonwy, the Princess of Llyr, when she is kidnapped and he must rescue her. He is aided by Prince Gwydion.

Alexander, Lloyd
A4
Tartan Wanderer
Holt, 1967

Taran is anxious to find out his real parentage but finds out a great deal about himself and his current position. He learns to weave, to forge a sword and to try sculpting clay.

Alexander, Lloyd
A5
High King
Holt, 1968

Taran and Prince Gwydion again battle the Land of Death lord, Arawn. Taran's quest for his heritage is ended and his future settled.

Alexander, Lloyd
B1
Illyrian Adventure
Dutton, 1986

Vesper, a 16-year-old orphan, researches an ancient legend and gets involved in a conspiracy to murder King Osman.

Alexander, Lloyd
B2
El Dorado Adventure
Dutton, 1987

Vesper stops a canal from being built that would destroy an Indian tribe homeland. Again evil Helvitius is foiled. This time by a volcano eruption.

Alexander, Lloyd
B3
Drackenberg Adventure
Dutton, 1988
 Vesper tangles with Dr. Helvitius, her number one enemy. He is looking for an art treasure.

Almedingen, E. M.
1
Young Mark
Farrar, 1967
 Mark sets on an adventure to fulfill his dreams of becoming a singer. This begins a four generation story of a remarkable family.

Almedingen, E. M.
2
Ellen
Farrar, 1970
 Mark's daughter is the main character in this next book. She marries the richest man in Russia.

Almedingen, E. M.
3
Fanny
Farrar, 1970
 Fanny is Ellen's daughter and Mark's granddaughter. The story of sophisticated and literary talented Frances de Poltratzky.

Almedingen, E. M.
4
Anna
Farrar, 1972
 Anna is the fourth generation daughter. She masters many languages, meets an empress and a handsome young man.

Armstrong, William
1
Sounder
Harper, 1969
 When his father is jailed for stealing food during hard times in the South, his young son and 'coon dog look for him in the chain gangs. He meets a former teacher who befriends him.

Armstrong, William
2

Sour Land
Harper, 1971
 The young boy grows up to be a teacher in the South where he finds both respect and injustice. A stark story of prejudice, rape and murder.

Arundel, Honor
1
High House
Meredith, 1967
 Emma and Richard are orphans who must be separated. Richard, who is musical, lives with the aunt who is very organized, and Emma, who likes a scheduled life is sent to the aunt who is musical.

Arundel, Honor
2
Emma's Island
Hawthorn, 1968
 Emma and her aunt and uncle move to a far-off island where, even though they are apprehensive, they adjust and learn to love the island and are glad of the change.

Arundel, Honor
3
Emma in Love
Nelson, 1970
 Emma and Richard are both back in London to go to school. Emma is in love with Alistair, a boy she met on the island, but he doesn't want to be pinned down and Emma loses perspective.

Arundel, Honor
A1
Terrible Temptation
Nelson, 1971
 Janet is determined to be independent and free from any personal involvements. This decision makes her appear cold and indifferent to the problems of others close to her.

Arundel, Honor
A2
Blanket Word
Nelson, 1973
 Janet's mother dies of cancer and Janet refuses to show any love or warm feelings, still determined to be indepen-

dent. But she tries to become understanding of what love means.

Asimov, Janet

1

Norby, the Mixed Up Robot

Walker, 1983

Jeff buys an old robot and names him Norby. Gidlow is the villain who wants to take over the world starting with Manhattan. Robots and dragons and rhyme talking computers fill out the story.

Asimov, Janet

2

Norby's Other Secret

Walker, 1984

The Inventor's Union wants Norby to dismantle and study. He and Jeff escape to Jamyn, a planet of friendly dragons, where Norby thinks he originated. He tells Jeff about his ability to travel through time.

Asimov, Janet

3

Norby and the Lost Princess

Walker, 1985

Norby the robot and Jeff his owner travel to the far-off planet of Izz. Their mission is to rescue a princess.

Asimov, Janet

4

Norby and the Invaders

Walker, 1985

Jeff and Norby go to Jamyn to aid Norby's ancestors. They visit another planet inhabited by creatures called Hleno.

Asimov, Janet

5

Norby and the Queen's Necklace

Walker, 1986

Jeff and his robot, Norby go back in time to 1785 in France. It is before the French Revolution and they might change history. Jeff must see that history is restored to normal.

Avi

1

Night Journey

Pantheon, 1979

Two indentured slaves, Elizabeth and Robert, are helped by Peter to escape in Pennsylvania. Mr. Shinn, a stern Quaker and Peter become closer companions during the ordeal.

Avi

2

Encounter in Easton

Pantheon, 1980

Robert and Elizabeth are helped by the Society of Friends when they escape to Pennsylvania. Bet tragically dies and Robert is servant to Mr. Hill who was involved in the death of Bet.

Babbit, Lucy

1

Oval Amulet

Harper, 1985

Paragrin and Cam begin an adventure in Melde. The Earth is inhabited by only one colony, and they are the rulers. They try their best to survive as a civilization.

Babbit, Lucy

2

Children of the Maker

Farrar, 1988

Paragrin and Cam are the rulers of Melde, supposedly the only colony on Earth. But there is another one, run by a rival sister.

Ball, Zachary

1

Bristle Face

Holiday, 1962

Jase, an orphan, and his dog, Bristle Face, make strong personal friendships with each other and Luke, a local store owner who wants to help.

Ball, Zachary

2

Sputters

Holiday, 1963

Jase and his new dog, Sputters, still continue to make friends and strong attachments to other people.

Ball, Zachary

A1

Joe Panther
Holiday, 1951
Joe is a Seminole Indian who is hired as a mate on a fishing boat. He saves a child's life and uncovers a ring of smugglers.

Ball, Zachary
A2
Skin Diver
Holiday, 1956
Joe now has his own fishing boat and is hired to explore the coral reefs. He has a narrow escape while being caught in the corals and also rescues a shipwrecked man.

Ballou, Arthur
1
Marooned in Orbit
Little, 1968
A spaceship is disabled as it orbits the moon, and the oxygen on board is running out.

Ballou, Arthur
2
Bound for Mars
Little, 1970
The spaceship, Pegasus, is scheduled to make man's first flight to Mars. Aboard is a team member who is a threat.

Beatty, Jerome
1
Bob Fulton's
Amazing Soda-Pop Stretcher
Scott, 1963
Bob tries to discover a way that he can quench every thirst in town. But he did not anticipate the problems connected with such an invention when it blew up and left a magic residue.

Beatty, Jerome
2
Bob Fulton's Terrific Time Machine
Scott, 1964
Bob is at it again with another invention. This time the machine he builds can change time. But, as usual, there are problems.

Beatty, Jerome
A1

Marie Looney on the Red Planet
Avon, 1977
Forces on both the earth and the moon fight the Moonsters and Marie.

Beatty, Jerome
A2
Marie Looney and the Cosmic Circus
Avon, 1978
More adventures with Marie and the Moonsters, taking place between the moon and earth.

Beatty, Jerome
A3
Marie Looney
and the Remarkable Robot
Avon, 1978
Marie is helped in her encounter with the Moonsters. This series ties into the Matthew Looney series, which also deals with the Moonsters.

Beatty, Jerome
B1
Matthew Looney's Voyage to the Earth
Avon, 1961
This story is told from the point of view of the moon-boy who comes to Earth to see if there is life there, and finds there is!

Beatty, Jerome
B2
Matthew Looney's
Invasion of the Earth
Wesley, 1965
Matt goes again to the Earth and then returns to the moon but this time in an American rocket ship because he missed his own ship that escaped the magic "rain."

Beatty, Jerome
B3
Matthew Looney in the Outback
Wesley, 1969
Matt knows of a plan of the Moonsters to destroy the Earth. He has to decide whether to save it or leave it to its doom. A lava bomb has been fired by the Moonsters.

Beatty, Jerome
B4

Matthew Looney and the Space Pirates
Wesley, 1972

Matt is captured by the Space Pirates while trying to establish a new planet. He is kept in a dungeon on Bolunkus.

Beatty, Patricia
1
Long Way to Whiskey Creek
Morrow, 1971

Nate, Parker Quimby and his dog, J.E.B. Stuart, travel far to bring back the body of a brother who was shot. They meet a Mexican witch, a medicine man, a gunslinger and an evangelist.

Beatty, Patricia
2
How Many Miles to Sundown?
Morrow, 1974

Beulah and Leo Quimby, along with Nate Graber, cross Texas and New Mexico in 1879 to look for Nate's missing father. They meet miners, outlaws and a traveling circus.

Beatty, Patricia
3
Billy Be Damned Long Gone By
Morrow, 1977

Rudd Quimby is a teller of tall tales as he reminisces about the past. His listeners soon realize this but still enjoy the stories.

Beatty, Patricia
A1
Turn Homeward, Hannalee
Morrow, 1984

Hannalee's life is disrupted when she is moved to Indiana with the rest of the Southern mill workers during the Civil War. She encounters Quantrill's Raiders and other horrors of war.

Beatty, Patricia
A2
Be Ever Hopeful, Hannalee
Morrow, 1988

Dave returns from the Civil War wounded. He is falsely arrested for murder. Hannalee must prove his innocence.

Bell, Clare
1

Ratha's Creatures
Atheneum, 1983

A clan of intelligent cats, pushed close to extinction, meets an enemy band of raiding predatory cats in a decisive battle which will determine the future of both.

Bell, Clare
2
Clan Ground
Atheneum, 1984

Twenty-five million years ago, the control of fire was power. Who will have this power, Ratha or her enemies? A dangerous struggle takes place, testing everyone's loyalty.

Bellairs, John
1
Curse of the Blue Figurine
Dial, 1983

John Dixon and Professor Childermass run into a mystery when John removes the blue figurine, called Shawabti, he was warned not to touch. A suspenseful, macabre tale.

Bellairs, John
2
Mummy, the Will and the Crypt
Dial, 1983

Again John Dixon and the Professor are mixed up in another mystery; this time involving the missing will of an eccentric old man who committed suicide.

Bellairs, John
3
Spell of the Sorcerer's Skull
Dial, 1984

A tiny skull from a haunted doll house unleashes demonic forces against John and Father Higgins. Professor Childermass is captured in this harrowing tale.

Bellairs, John
4
Revenge of the Wizard's Ghost
Dial, 1985

Johnny Dixon lies dying, hexed by the evil spirit of Warren Winslow. The Professor and his friends try to save him.

Bellairs, John
5
Eyes of the Killer Robot
Dial, 1986

Johnny Dixon and Professor Childermass look for a baseball pitching robot made many years ago by a wizard. He may be evil when found and reassembled.

Bellairs, John
A1
House with a Clock in Its Walls
Dial, 1973

Lewis and his wizard uncle, Jonathan, use magic and terror to solve the mystery of the clock set to destroy the world.

Bellairs, John
A2
Figure in the Shadows
Dial, 1975

This time an old coin starts the sinister events that lead Lewis and his friend, Rose, to solve another mystery involving ghosts and other evils.

Bellairs, John
A3
Letter, the Witch and the Ring
Dial, 1976

Lewis' friend, Rose, goes with Jonathan's neighbor, Mrs. Zimmermann, who is a witch, to a farmhouse to solve a mystery that even Mrs. Zimmermann's witchcraft can't help.

Bellairs, John
B1
Treasure of Alpheus Winterborn
Harcourt, 1978

Anthony Monday looks for a treasure rumored to be hidden in his hometown library. He and Miss Eels work together and find a clue in the fireplace.

Bellairs, John
B2
Dark Secret of Weatherend
Dial, 1984

Anthony Monday tries to stop a wicked wizard from turning the Earth to ice. Wizard Borkman can control the weather and leaves the formula to his son, Anders.

Bellairs, John
B3
Lamp from Warlock's Tomb
Dial, 1988

Anthony Monday recovers the lamp that is spreading evil throughout the world. Miss Eels bought the lamp at an antique sale and strange things happen. It once belonged to Willis Nightwood.

Benary-Isbert, Margot
1
Ark
Harcourt, 1953

The ark is an abandoned railroad car in which the Lechow family live after escaping from a Russian prison camp. Matthias and Margaret are glad to be together even though they lost a brother.

Benary-Isbert, Margot
2
Rowan Farm
Harcourt, 1954

Rowan farm is where the "Ark" becomes home for the Lechow family and where they farm. Margaret finds peace and quiet among the animals, especially with the dogs.

Benary-Isbert, Margot
3
Castle on the Border
Harcourt, 1956

The Lechow family adjusts after World War II and faces the future with hope and strength. Leni wants to become a great actress and overcome her tragic war-life with love.

Best, Herbert
1
Desmond's First Case
Viking, 1961

Desmond (dog) and Gus (boy) look for the dissappeared Mr. Titus, friend, neighbor and ex-banker. The search is told by the dog from his point of view.

Best, Herbert
2
Desmond the Dog Detective
Viking, 1962

A jumble of happenings, mainly in

the supermarket where Desmond is looking for a thief behind the dog food boxes, again told by Desmond as he ᴄᴏᴏᴄ ᵢₜ

Best, Herbert
3
Desmond and the Peppermint Ghost
Viking, 1965

Desmond now tells about learning how dogs pull sleds. By following a scent of peppermint Desmond leads Gus to an empty house and the answers about the ghost.

Best, Herbert
4
Desmond and Dog Friday
Viking, 1968

Desmond is joined by an Hungarian Puli named Friday. Friday digs up a bone from an early Indian cache. Again Desmond is the detective with savvy and solves the mystery.

Bethancourt, T. E.
Pr1
Dr. Doom, Superstar
Holiday, 1978

Doris Fein is only a minor character in this story but it is our introduction to this sleuthing heroine. Larry Small interviews a Rock star. There is a death threat and the mystery begins.

Bethancourt, T. E.
1
Doris Fein, Superspy
Holiday, 1978

Doris is a super sleuth just out of high school and starts an adventure in New York when her aunt and uncle get a mysterious call to go to Africa where trouble is brewing.

Bethancourt, T. E.
2
Doris Fein, Quartz Boyar
Holiday, 1980

Doris feels she has had enough of detective work and goes to Paris on holiday only to become involved in an international adventure because of a quartz figurine.

Bethancourt, T. E.
3
Doris Fein, Phantom of the Casino
Scholastic, 1981

This time, in Santa Catalina, Doris finds that her death is the revenge wanted by the "phantom." She has a romantic episode and lots of adventure.

Bethancourt, T. E.
4
Doris Fein, Mad Samurai
Scholastic, 1981

As Doris investigates the murder of two people allegedly killed by Samurai swordsmen, she finds her own life in danger.

Bethancourt, T. E.
5
Doris Fein, Deadly Aphrodite
Holiday, 1982

Doris and her friend, Larry Small, try to solve an old mystery where someone is systematically doing away with the world's wealthiest women at an exclusive spa.

Bethancourt, T. E.
6
Doris Fein, Murder Is No Joke
Holiday, 1982

This mystery starts in a Southern California night club where her new friend is found to be a killer, and moves to Las Vegas and encounters with organized crime.

Bethancourt, T. E.
7
Doris Fein, Dead Heat at Long Beach
Holiday, 1983

A racing car driver and Doris get involved with revolutionaries. Even Doris must use her driving skills to survive this encounter with guerrillas and offshore oil intrigue.

Bethancourt, T. E.
8
Doris Fein, Legacy of Terror
Holiday, 1983

A 15-million-dollar inheritance, a kidnapping and organized crime are the source of terror for Doris.

Bethancourt, T. E.
A1
Tune in Yesterday
Holiday, 1978
   Two boys enter a one-way door to the past. They are in New York City, 1942. It was fun until the threat of World War II began. They are kidnapped and escape. They jump through another door into 1912.

Bethancourt, T. E.
A2
Tomorrow Connection
Holiday, 1984
   Two musicians are stranded in San Francisco in 1906 and enlist Harry Houdini to help them find a way to their future.

Blume, Judy
1
Otherwise Known as Sheila the Great
Dutton, 1972
   Peter finds out that Sheila is afraid of dogs, bees, water, noises, etc.

Blume, Judy
2
Tales of a Fourth Grade Nothing
Dutton, 1972
   Peter is the younger brother of Fudge. Among other things Fudge swallows Peter's pet turtle. Peter has a friend in Sheila.

Blume, Judy
3
Superfudge
Dutton, 1980
   Fudge's life is a mess. He moves from New York to New Jersey. He gets a baby sister called Tootsie. And he doesn't like either event.

Bodker, Cecil
1
Silas and the Black Mare
Delacorte, 1967
   Silas overcomes several problems to keep the splendid mare he has won from a greedy horse trainer.

Bodker, Cecil
2
Silas and Ben Godik
Delacorte, 1978
   Silas and Ben Godik spend a year traveling by horseback and encounter many strange and harrowing adventures including rescuing a young boy who has been kidnapped.

Bodker, Cecil
3
Silas and the Runaway Coach
Delacorte, 1978
   Silas still has many adventures even though he is now living with a very rich family and learns manners and reading. He and the family's son are kidnapped by an old enemy of Silas'.

Bond, Michael
1
Bear Called Paddington
Houghton, 1958
   A bear, who lives with the Brown's gets in all kinds of mischief.

Bond, Michael
2
More About Paddington
Houghton, 1962
   In this story Paddington decides to redo the room the Brown's gave him as his own.

Bond, Michael
3
Paddington Helps Out
Houghton, 1960
   Paddington wants to help with the household chores but when he enters the laundry room, there's chaos.

Bond, Michael
4
Paddington at Large
Houghton, 1962
   Now Paddington is going to help mow the lawn but somehow he loses control of the lawn mower and again there's chaos.

Bond, Michael
5
Paddington Marches On
Houghton, 1964
   Paddington is determined to go to

work. He tries several jobs—but a bear in a marmalade factory!!!

Bond, Michael
6
Paddington at Work
Houghton, 1967
After visiting Peru, Paddington is ready to get back to work.

Bond, Michael
7
Paddington Goes to Town
Houghton, 1968
Now Paddington is taking to cooking. But his deserts are not what they are cracked up to be.

Bond, Michael
8
Paddington Takes the Air
Houghton, 1970
Troubles again for Paddington as he meets crisis after crisis.

Bond, Michael
9
Paddington Abroad
Houghton, 1972
Map and language troubles are Paddington's concern now.

Bond, Michael
10
Paddington Takes to T.V.
Houghton, 1972
Paddington wins a baking contest and goes on television.

Bond, Michael
11
Paddington on Top
Houghton, 1974
Paddington has troubles on his first, and last, day in school.

Bond, Michael
12
Paddington Takes the Test
Houghton, 1980
A driving test for Paddington. Heaven Forbid!!

Bond, Michael
13
Paddington on Screen

Houghton, 1982
Paddington is a television star, but his mishaps follow him wherever he goes.

Bond, Nancy
1
Best of Enemies
Atheneum, 1978
Charlotte experiences a celebration that does not go as planned. The Patriot's Day reenactment is perhaps too real.

Bond, Nancy
2
Place to Come Back to
Atheneum, 1984
When Charlotte's friend, Oliver, is saddened by the death of his guardian, he turns to Charlotte who must make decisions and face responsibilities she doesn't want.

Bonham, Frank
1
Mystery of the Fat Cat
Dutton, 1968
A "counterfeit" cat (Is it really Buzzer Adkins?) holds the key to saving the Oak Street Boys Club in Dogtown for its four main members.

Bonham, Frank
2
Nitty-Gritty
Dutton, 1968
A bright, young Black, Charlie, wants to continue school but his father wants him to quit. An uncle comes to his aid but Charlie, living in Dogtown, still has difficult decisions to make.

Bonham, Frank
3
Vivi Chicano
Dutton, 1970
Keeny, a young Mexican–American (Chicano), unwillingly breaks parole and must hide because of unjust accusations.

Bonham, Frank
4
Cool Cat
Dutton, 1971

Buddy, who also lives in Dogtown, needs money to buy a much wanted and needed scooter. He listens to a newcomer to Dogtown about how to make money faster than at a part-time job.

Bonham, Frank
5
Hey, Big Spender
Dutton, 1972
Cool can't believe he has a summer job of giving away a million dollars. He tries to separate out the families who are most in need. He thinks there should be no problems.

Boston, Lucy
1
Children of Green Knowe
Harcourt, 1955
Tolly is a lonesome youngster living with his great-grandmother in an old house. But with the aid of his imagination he is able to find exciting adventures.

Boston, Lucy
2
Treasure of Green Knowe
Harcourt, 1958
Granny tells Tolly stories as she works on her patchwork quilt. They learn of a treasure which has been missing for over a generation and begin to look for it.

Boston, Lucy
3
River of Green Knowe
Harcourt, 1959
Three youngsters come to Green Knowe and, left to their own resources, explore the fascinating river in a canoe they found. Reality and fantasy merge as they move through their adventure.

Boston, Lucy
4
Stranger at Green Knowe
Harcourt, 1961
Ping, one of the three children who stayed at Green Knowe, befriends an escaped gorilla who finds his way to Green Knowe.

Boston, Lucy
5
Enemy of Green Knowe
Harcourt, 1964
Tolly and Ping are involved in a mystery that might harm Green Knowe when black magic from an old alchemist's book of magic is searched for.

Boston, Lucy
6
Stones of Green Knowe
Atheneum, 1976
Roger, whose family once owned Green Knowe, is able to travel back and forth through time with the help of two magical stones he found.

Boston, Lucy
7
Guardians of the House
Atheneum, 1974
Tom goes into the old house that was known as Green Knowe. He finds a lot of old carved masks and his adventure begins.

Boylston, Helen
1
Sue Barton, Student Nurse
Little, 1936
This is the first year of Sue's training as a nurse. Her two friends, Kit and Connie help her get through the probationary period in spite of all her humorous mistakes. She moves on from here.

Boylston, Helen
2
Sue Barton, Senior Nurse
Little, 1937
She finishes training and is at a hospital where she meets interesting people. There is a minor mystery and some setbacks with the Head Nurse.

Boylston, Helen
3
Sue Barton, Visiting Nurse
Little, 1938
Sue Barton is the visiting nurse at the Henry Street Settlement in New York.

Boylston, Helen
4

Sue Barton, Rural Nurse
Little, 1939

In this book, Sue's romance with Dr. Barry is deepening. Her career is moving forward.

Boylston, Helen
5
Sue Barton, Superintendent of Nurses
Little, 1940

Sue Barton establishes a training school for nurses. She marries Dr. Barry and resigns her position to stay home and be a wife and mother.

Boylston, Helen
6
Sue Barton, Neighborhood Nurse
Little, 1949

Sue is married and has three children. Her husband is head of a hospital. She begins to pick up her career again.

Boylston, Helen
7
Sue Barton, Staff Nurse
Little, 1952

Although married with children of her own, Sue feels she should be using her training to help others so she continues to help in the hospital.

Branscum, Robbie
1
Toby, Granny and George
Doubleday, 1976

Toby is an orphan left on the steps of Granny's house. George is her dog. Strange things are happening in the Arkansas hills surrounding Granny's home and Toby learns about love and caring.

Branscum, Robbie
2
Toby Alone
Doubleday, 1979

Granny dies and Toby is left alone and does not cope well with those who want to help her. She likes Johnny Joe but puts him off, too.

Branscum, Robbie
3
Toby and Johnny Joe
Doubleday, 1979

Toby grows up and solves the conflict between herself and Johnny Joe. They get married before he goes off to war. Tragedy upon tragedy hamper both Toby and Johnny Joe.

Branscum, Robbie
A1
Johnny May
Doubleday, 1975

The story of a young girl growing up in Arkansas while living with a grandmother. She is resourceful and imaginative.

Branscum, Robbie
A2
Adventures of Johnny May
Harper, 1984

Johnny May, 11, shows a great deal of responsibility in taking care of her ailing grandparents. Does she see a murder? Her guilt about killing a deer is eased by the man she saw.

Branscum, Robbie
A3
Johnny May Grows Up
Harper, 1987

Johnny May tries many self-improvement tricks to impress her boyfriend, Aaron, but finds that it is important to herself regardless of what others think.

Branson, Karen
1
Potatoe Eaters
Putnam, 1979

The O'Conner family left Ireland during the famine and came to New York. The mother remained behind and will join her family later. One member of the family has already died.

Branson, Karen
2
Streets of Gold
Putnam, 1981

The O'Conner family realizes that just being in New York is not going to solve their problems. They have family stress problems when jobs can't be found but they persevere.

Brink, Carol
1
Caddie Woodlawn
Macmillan, 1935
Caddie and her family have a difficult time eking out a living in pioneer Wisconsin but she and her brother make their life tolerable by having adventures in the open wilderness.

Brink, Carol
2
Magical Melons
Macmillan, 1944
This collection of stories about Caddie and her brothers tells of their many adventures, some safe and funny and some with dire consequences.

Brink, Carol
A1
Family Grandstand
Viking, 1952
The Ridgeway family, Susan, 12, George, 11, and Dumpling, 7, plus mother and father, the Professor, live near Midwest University. This story is of one football season and all its fascination.

Brink, Carol
A2
Family Sabbatical
Viking, 1956
Again the Ridgeway family a year or so later. They are in France where the children teach their tutor more English than she teaches them French. Lots of exciting and funny adventures.

Brink, Carol
B1
Two Are Better Than One
Macmillan, 1968
Chrystal and Cordelia are best friends. They write a book about their dolls but it is really a dream of their own.

Brink, Carol
B2
Louly
Macmillan, 1974
Chrys, Cordy, Louly and Ko-Ko camp in a tent in the backyard. Louly is taking care of them and they have a very good time.

Brittain, Bill
1
Devil's Donkey
Harper, 1981
Lots of magic with even more humor as Old Magda, the witch, practices her strange antics. Dan'l Pitt offended Old Magda and is turned into a donkey. Eventually he does get turned back.

Brittain, Bill
2
Wish Giver
Harper, 1983
Wishes are made and granted in this follow-up story of Old Magda, the witch, Dan'l Pitt and Stew Meat (Steward Meade). It, too, takes place in Coven Tree.

Brittain, Bill
3
Dr. Dread's Wagon of Wonders
Harper, 1987
Dr. Dread, a companion to the Devil, makes the townspeople of Coven Tree very greedy. But honesty prevails and he is reduced to dust. When the drought continues the rainmaker is brought in.

Brooks, Walter
1
Freddy the Detective
Knopf, 1932
Freddy solves the mystery of the missing toy train.

Brooks, Walter
2
Freddy and the Ignormus
Knopf, 1941
Freddy and his friends do awful things to rid the Bean farm of the fearful Ignormus who has been terrifying all the animals.

Brooks, Walter
3
Freddy and the Perilous Adventure
Knopf, 1942
Freddy goes up in a balloon at the Fair. He looked forward to going and

had a wonderful time with his friends, the ducks and the spider.

Brooks, Walter
4
Freddy and the Bean Home News
Knopf, 1943
Freddy plans a rival newspaper with himself as editor.

Brooks, Walter
5
Freddy and Mr. Camphor
Knopf, 1944
Freddy is caretaker of the estate of wealthy Mr. Camphor, while there some old enemies reappear: Simon the rat and Mr. Winch and his son, Horace.

Brooks, Walter
6
Freddy and the Popinjay
Knopf, 1945
Freddy almost loses his tail so he fits J.J. Pomeroy, the Robin, with glasses.

Brooks, Walter
7
Freddy and the Pied Piper
Knopf, 1946
Freddy is called on to advise in a circus. He plays the role of the Pied Piper to call the scattered animals of the circus together.

Brooks, Walter
8
Freddy the Magician
Knopf, 1947
Freddy is a magician and gets the best of the Machiavellian circus magician in the end.

Brooks, Walter
9
Freddy Goes Camping
Knopf, 1948
Freddy stumbles onto a mystery. Someone is dressing as a ghost and haunting the occupants of a hotel. He and his friends lead that someone on a merry chase.

Brooks, Walter
10
Freddy the Politician
Knopf, 1948
When the Bean farm animals form the First Animal Republic Freddie fights for rights against the rats and the woodpeckers.

Brooks, Walter
11
Freddy Goes to Florida
Knopf, 1949
The hero is Freddy the pig. All the farm animals decide to escape the cold winter by going to Florida.

Brooks, Walter
12
Freddy Plays Football
Knopf, 1949
Freddy is pushed into a football game by mistake and plays well. He becomes a member of the team. And meanwhile solves another mystery.

Brooks, Walter
13
Freddy Goes to the North Pole
Knopf, 1951
Freddy is off again on one of his many trips, playing out one of his many roles. We'll find him home again and off again in this series of books.

Brooks, Walter
14
Freddy the Cowboy
Knopf, 1951
Freddy rescues Cy, a horse, from Mr. Flint. So now he learns to ride and to shoot.

Brooks, Walter
15
Freddy Rides Again
Knopf, 1951
Freddy comes through his exploits with Mr. Elihu P. Margarine, a wealthy fox hunter and another menace, a rattlesnake, in a blaze of glory.

Brooks, Walter
16
Freddy the Pilot
Knopf, 1952
Mr. Bean buys Freddy an airplane. He outwits the villain who employs air

bombs to reach his goal: the attention of the bareback rider.

Brooks, Walter
17
Freddy and the Space Ship
Knopf, 1953
Freddy's trip aboard a spaceship takes off and lands on Earth. Freddy colors himself blue and finds out about the duck's stolen jewels and rids the Bean farm of unwanted relatives.

Brooks, Walter
18
Freddy and the Men from Mars
Knopf, 1954
The circus has phoney "Men from Mars." Freddy finds this out. The "real" Martians come to investigate and help Freddy put everything right.

Brooks, Walter
19
Freddy and the Baseball Team from Mars
Knopf, 1955
The circus lost one of its Martians and Freddy goes to investigate. The outcome is that he was made coach of the baseball team as well as solving the mystery.

Brooks, Walter
20
Freddy and the Dictator
Knopf, 1956
There is a revolt at Bean farm and Freddy is in the middle of it.

Brooks, Walter
21
Freddy and the Flying Saucer Plans
Knopf, 1957
Freddy helps Uncle Ben save his flying saucer plans from spies.

Brooks, Walter
22
Freddy and the Dragon
Knopf, 1958
Freddy is unpopular when a crime wave hits town. All the evidence points toward animals being the culprits.

Burch, Robert
1
Ida Early Comes Over the Mountain
Atheneum, 1980
Ida arrives at the Sutton home at just the right time. She is an extraordinary housekeeper and cook and the children like her. However, they have a lot to learn about loyalty.

Burch, Robert
2
Christmas with Ida Early
Atheneum, 1983
Ida Early becomes the target of the children's matchmaking schemes. During a Christmas pageant Ida livens up the play. Ida and the new preacher have different opinions about what happened.

Burch, Robert
A1
Tyler, Wilkins and Skee
Viking, 1963
Three brothers live on a farm in the South. With a strict but fair father they get all their chores done before fun. Wilkins and Tyler are friendly toward Alex, who steals and then runs away.

Burch, Robert
A2
Wilkin's Ghost
Viking, 1978
Wilkin has a friend, Alex, who is a runaway accused of stealing. Wilkin tries to help and almost gets into trouble himself before he realizes that Alex is a phoney.

Burton, Hester
1
Rebel
Crowell, 1971
Stephen, an idealistic radical who cares for the poor and oppressed, goes to Paris instead of to his uncle's home in England. He is caught up in the French Revolution and is imprisoned.

Burton, Hester
2
Riders of the Storm
Crowell, 1973

Stephen is freed from the French prison and returns to England where he continues his work with the poor and down-trodden. He is accused of being a government conspirator.

Butler, Beverly
1
Light a Single Candle
Dodd, 1962

A story of Cathy's adjustment to blindness. She lost her sight at age 14. She has a seeing eye dog and great support from her family, her teachers and her friends.

Butler, Beverly
2
Gift of Gold
1972

Cathy is a blind college student and is told there is some hope for partially-returned eyesight.

Byrd, Elizabeth
1
I'll Get By
Viking, 1981

Although Julie seemed to have all a girl could want including success in school, what she really wants is her absent father to return, and have a normal two-parent family.

Byrd, Elizabeth
2
It Had to Be You
Viking, 1982

Julie's friends, Marge and Kitty, are affected by the Great Depression. Julie wants to become an actress, and Marge to be a social success. Both are optimistic, romantic dreamers.

Calhoun, Mary
1
Katie John
Harper, 1960

Katie John is an irresistible young girl who moves into an inherited house with her family. They intend to sell the house but after living there for a while, they decide to stay.

Calhoun, Mary
2
Depend on Katie John
Harper, 1961

Katie John and her family live in their 20-room inherited house where they rent out some rooms. This makes their lives change some.

Calhoun, Mary
3
Honestly Katie John
Harper, 1963

Katie John is president of the "Boy Haters of America" club. She also goes to see a fortune teller.

Calhoun, Mary
4
Katie John and Heathcliff
Harper, 1980

The one-time boy-hater Katie John falls in love with Jason. He is lured away by Trish, a country club type. But she finds old friend Edwin more interesting anyway.

Callen, Larry
1
Pinch
Little, 1975

Pinch lives by his wits, he feels that's the only way to survive. He turns a found quarter into an adventure which realizes him a pig for which his father has a different set of plans.

Callen, Larry
2
Deadly Mandrake
Little, 1978

Pinch's town of Four Corners appears to be cursed by an evil spirit. Pinch and his friend, Sorrow, are going to uproot the mandrake growing in the cemetery and stop the curse.

Callen, Larry
3
Sorrow's Song
Little, 1979

Sorrow, a mute, finds a crane and wants to protect it from being caged. She believes in freedom for all creatures. She and Pinch do their best to help the bird.

Callen, Larry
4
Muskrat War
Little, 1980

Winter is to be long and hard for Pinch and his father so he and his friend Charley are trapping and hiding muskrat hides. But swindlers trick them; they must catch them and recover the hides.

Cameron, Eleanor
1
Julia's Magic
Dutton, 1984

Julia needs to see that "honesty is the best policy." She learns a lesson when another person is about to be harmed by Julia's unreported, and partially covered, accident.

Cameron, Eleanor
2
That Julia Redfern
Dutton, 1982

Julia wants to become a writer. She has to cope with her mother and aunt because her father, who believes in her, has gone away to fight in the war.

Cameron, Eleanor
3
Julia and the Hand of God
Dutton, 1977

Julia wants to be a writer. Uncle Hugh gives her a new book full of empty pages for her to write "her impressions." She finds putting feelings into words is not easy.

Cameron, Eleanor
4
Room Made of Windows
Little, 1971

Julia aspires to be a great writer but she must go beyond her window, which she has used as an observation point, to a bigger world where love and compassion and reality exists.

Cameron, Eleanor
5
Private World of Julia Redfern
Dutton, 1988

Julia's uncle and grandmother help her through some tight moments of jealousy but she learns to forgive and love. She also experiences some artistic satisfaction.

Cameron, Eleanor
A1
*Wonderful Flight
to the Mushroom Planet*
Little, 1954

Two boys, David and Chuck, help Mr. Bass build a spaceship and then they take off in it to Basidium and help the people there by adding (See Title) to their daily diet.

Cameron, Eleanor
A2
Stowaway to the Mushroom Planet
Little, 1956

Basidium must be kept a secret from the general public so that it can remain unharmed. But on the next trip there Chuck and David find a stowaway on board, Horatio Q. Peabody!

Cameron, Eleanor
A3
Mr. Bass's Planetoid
Little, 1958

With Mr. Bass away from Earth, Chuck and David must investigate Mr. Brumblydge's new invention. They look through Mr. Bass's notes and end up following Mr. Brumblydge to Lepton.

Cameron, Eleanor
A4
Mystery for Mr. Bass
Little, 1960

Mr. Brumblydge needs the help of the King of the Mushroom Planet, Ta, to recover from a strange ailment. Chuck and David get him and cope with new scientific discoveries.

Cameron, Eleanor
A5
Time and Mr. Bass
Little, 1967

This mystery involves an ancient scroll and the Necklace of Ta that has been stolen and, of course, Mr. Bass's travel through time, so that he might defeat the evil powers.

Cameron, Eleanor
B1
Terrible Churnadryne
Little, 1959
Tom and Jennifer went to find the monster on San Lorenzo hill. What did they really see in the fog? Would people believe them? Was it a prehistoric monster?

Cameron, Eleanor
B2
Mysterious Christmas Shell
Little, 1961
Tom and Jennifer learn a lesson about tradition and the importance of preserving old things.

Canning, Victor
1
Runaways
Morrow, 1971
Smiler runs away and stays in a deserted barn with his new friend, a runaway cheetah.

Canning, Victor
2
Flight of the Grey Goose
Morrow, 1973
When Smiler is older he runs away again, this time to await the return of his father.

Carlson, Natalie
1
Half Sisters
Harper, 1970
Luvvy can't wait for her half-sister to return from boarding school so she can display how much she has grown up and changed. She is 12 and no longer a tomboy.

Carlson, Natalie
2
Luvvy and the Girls
Harper, 1971
Luvvy is thrilled by the fact that she, too, can go to boarding school. This is her first year and she finds the day-by-day activities adventurous.

Carlson, Natalie
A1

Happy Orphelines
Harper, 1957
The story of 20 girls who live in an orphanage in France and don't want to be adopted. It is the first of many funny tales. Because of a pending adoption they act very badly to prevent it.

Carlson, Natalie
A2
Brother for the Orphelines
Harper, 1959
A foundling is left at the door of the Orphelines, but it is a boy! They care for him and struggle to keep him even if it is an orphanage for girls.

Carlson, Natalie
A3
Pet for the Orphelines
Harper, 1962
The Orphelines can identify with unwanted, homeless cats. Their sympathetic approach is warm and understanding. But they do have difficulty deciding on what kind of pet they want.

Carlson, Natalie
A4
Orphelines in the Enchanted Castle
Harper, 1964
Another adventure of the girls from the orphanage when they go to live in a castle where there will be orphan boys. Their first ideas about boys change as the boys tease and misbehave.

Carlson, Natalie
A5
Grandmother for the Orphelines
Harper, 1980
The Orphelines find not only a grandmother but a grandfather too, and on Christmas Eve!

Carroll, Lewis
1
Alice's Adventures in Wonderland
1865
Alice falls down a rabbit hole and discovers a world of characters who are nonsensical, funny, wicked and compassionate.

Carroll, Lewis
2
Through the Looking Glass
1871
Alice goes through a looking glass this time and finds a different world full of curious adventures.

Chaikin, Miriam
1
I Should Worry, I Should Care
Harper, 1979
The story of Molly and her sisters and brother as they move into a new neighborhood and must adjust to school and new friends. Death, poverty and anti–Semitism is part of their lives.

Chaikin, Miriam
2
Finders Weepers
Harper, 1980
Molly finds a ring and keeps it but when she finds out its significance she wants to give it back but can't get it off her finger.

Chaikin, Miriam
3
Getting Even
Harper, 1982
Molly learns about friendship, betrayal and jealousy as she makes friends and knows of the responsibility of this act.

Chaikin, Miriam
4
Lower! Higher! You're a Liar!
Harper, 1984
Molly's best friend is gone for the summer. She befriends Estelle who is a victim of Celia, the school bully, who takes her bracelet. Molly organizes a club to boycott Celia.

Chambers, John
1
Finder
Atheneum, 1981
A dog found Jenny when she arrived at Fire Island for the summer. The dog belonged to another boy and Jenny and her friend, Lauren, come upon a mystery and a kidnapping.

Chambers, John
2
Showdown at Apple Hill
Atheneum, 1982
Jenny and her brother, Bill, run into the Quarry gang of robbers and murderers. They are looking for the loot that was hidden there 12 years before.

Chambers, John
3
Fire Island Forfeit
Atheneum, 1984
Jenny, her brother, Bill and her girlfriend, Lauren, investigate a mystery of Fire Island. Lione, a model, is murdered. She is the same girl that gave Lauren a box with keys in it.

Chance, Stephen
1
Septimus and Danedyke Mystery
Nelson, 1971
A pastor finds himself in danger when some manuscripts are discovered showing where a golden cup is hidden that two art thieves are looking for.

Chance, Stephen
2
Septimus and the Minister Ghost Mystery
Nelson, 1974
Rev. Treivar sees unexplained lights, hears organ music and the talking of ghosts. He and Alistair go to investigate the old church.

Chance, Stephen
3
Stone Offering
Nelson, 1977
When a valley is threatened by plans for building a dam, someone tries to save his home by reenacting an ancient magic formula.

Christopher, John
Pr1
When the Tripods Came
Dutton, 1988
This is a prequel. This is the story of how the Tripods came to be and how they gained control. It leaves off where *White Mountains* begins.

Christopher, John
1
White Mountains
Macmillan, 1967
In a future world where tripods control the minds of all, three boys, Will, Henry and Beanpole make a break for freedom by fleeing to the White Mountains.

Christopher, John
2
City of Gold and Lead
Macmillan, 1967
Will, Fritz and Beanpole go to the City of the Tripod to learn what they can about their ability to rule the Earth the way they do.

Christopher, John
3
Pool of Fire
Macmillan, 1968
Will, Henry and Beanpole must foil the Master's plan of world domination.

Christopher, John
A1
Fireball
Dutton, 1981
When the fireball comes, this huge whirling ball of light causes everything to be terrifyingly different. The land is made up of two worlds, one past and one future. Simon and Brad are in both.

Christopher, John
A2
New Found Land
Dutton, 1983
In their attempt to reach California, Brad and Simon, one American and one Englishman, face Vikings, Indians and Aztecs.

Christopher, John
A3
Dragon Dance
Dutton, 1986
Loyal Simon and know-it-all Brad are now in China where they experience mind-control practices and palatial intrigue. In the end of this trilogy they do come home.

Christopher, John
B1
Prince in Waiting
Macmillan, 1970
Luke survives the Earth's volcanic eruption, but civilization, with its technology is destroyed. Luke must fight the Seers and bring back machinery.

Christopher, John
B2
Beyond the Burning Land
Macmillan, 1971
Luke is waiting for the time to fulfill the Spirit's plans for restoration of the machine age. He slays a monster and wins a princess. He then becomes Prince of Winchester.

Christopher, John
B3
Sword of the Spirits
Macmillan, 1972
Luke does not have a peaceful time as Prince. He faces a mutiny of his captains and is exiled. He does return and tries to reintroduce machines into his society.

Christopher, John
C1
Wild Jack
Macmillan, 1974
Intrigue and adventure in the twenty-third century, Olive escapes to the Outlands and is befriended by Wild Jack and his gang. This is said to be the first of a new trilogy, but where is two?

Christopher, Matt
1
Dog that Stole the Football Plays
Little, 1980
Mike listens while his telepathic dog transmits the opposing team's signals. When Harry, the dog, gets sick the team must win without that kind of "cheating."

Christopher, Matt
2
Dog that Called the Signals
Little, 1982
During a football game, Harry, the

dog calls plays from the home of the sick coach.

Christopher, Matt
3
Dog that Pitched a No-Hitter
Little, 1988

Mike's telepathic dog, Harry, is sending his usual signals but Mike's pitching is so bad they must try another plan.

Church, Richard
1
Five Boys in a Cave
Day, 1950

Five boys investigate a cave. Two boys are let down by a rope to a lower cave and face terror when the rope is dropped. A way out must be found.

Church, Richard
2
Down River
Day, 1957

Five boys search a cave for ancient Roman remains. But another group is searching also. And smugglers are there, too, looking for the same thing.

Clarke, Mary
1
Iron Peacock
Viking, 1966

Ross McCrae, a Scottish prisoner and Joanna, 16 and fleeing from Cromwell, try to build a new life in early America. They are bound to the Iron Master.

Clarke, Mary
2
Piper to the Clan
Viking, 1970

When Cromwell beats the Scots some of them are sent as prisoners to America to work as laborers. Ross is among them. He was piper of his clan and feels the loss greatly.

Cleary, Beverly
1
Beezus and Ramona
Morrow, 1955

Sibling rivalry between Ramona and her sister Beezus. Beezus is constantly embarrassed by Ramona's antics.

Cleary, Beverly
2
Ramona the Pest
Morrow, 1968

Ramona is a very funny little girl. Like a lot of other little girls she means to do well but some how everything ends up wrong. She is discouraged.

Cleary, Beverly
3
Ramona the Brave
Morrow, 1975

Ramona and Beezus are members of a very unusual family. Ramona thinks she is doing everything right but Beezus is still embarrassed by her and her teacher is exasperated.

Cleary, Beverly
4
Ramona and Her Father
Morrow, 1977

Ramona Quimby's father loses his job but the story of this family is always funny regardless of circumstances. Mrs. Quimby gets a job in the meantime.

Cleary, Beverly
5
Ramona and Her Mother
Morrow, 1979

Now both of Ramona's parents are working and she must be baby-sat. Ramona doesn't like any of this.

Cleary, Beverly
6
Ramona Quimby, Age 8
Morrow, 1981

Mr. Quimby is training for a new career and Ramona is training to become a model student.

Cleary, Beverly
7
Ramona Forever
Morrow, 1984

There are big family changes that make Ramona's life very different. Mrs. Quimby is going to have a baby and Mr. Quimby is still having employment problems. On top of that, the cat dies.

Cleary, Beverly
A1
Mouse and the Motorcycle
Morrow, 1965

A humorous fantasy about a wild mouse name Ralph. He sees Keith playing with a motorcycle and decides he'd like to do that.

Cleary, Beverly
A2
Runaway Ralph
Morrow, 1970

Ralph runs away to a children's camp for a life of speed, danger and excitement. Garf, his new "owner" must save him from disaster.

Cleary, Beverly
A3
Ralph S. Mouse
Morrow, 1982

Ralph still lives in the hotel and befriends a newcomer, Ryan. Since all his many relatives want to ride his motorcycle, Ralph goes to school with Ryan and becomes famous.

Cleary, Beverly
B1
Henry Huggins
Morrow, 1950

Henry has been given the lead part in the school Christmas play. To him, it was too horrible to even think about. But his adopted stray dog, Ribsy, is also causing trouble.

Cleary, Beverly
B2
Henry and Beezus
Morrow, 1952

Henry wants a new bike. But before he can get it he must deal with his dog, Ribsy, who is into mischief; his friend Beezus, who tries to help and Ramona, Beezus' sister, the pest.

Cleary, Beverly
B3
Henry and Ribsy
Morrow, 1954

Henry and his dog, Ribsy get in and out of a great deal of predicaments.

Cleary, Beverly
B4
Henry and the Paper Route
Morrow, 1957

Henry wants a paper route but he is too young. He helps his friend fold papers and substitutes for him when he is sick. He doesn't get a route when one opens, it is given to someone else.

Cleary, Beverly
B5
Henry and the Clubhouse
Morrow, 1962

Beezus and Ramona cause no end of trouble for Henry and his dog, Ribsy.

Cleaver, Vera
1
Where the Lilies Bloom
Lippincott, 1969

The death of Mary Call's father poses a problem since she promised to bury him secretly and take care of the family so that they would not become welfare cases.

Cleaver, Vera
2
Trial Valley
Lippincott, 1977

Mary Call is still caring for her brothers and sisters, but has two rival suitors. She must make some hard decisions including what to do about the abandoned boy, Jack Parsons.

Cleaver, Vera
A1
Ellen Grae
Lippincott, 1967

Ellen stays with Mrs. McGruder and tells lies. Her friends are young Grover and retarded old Ira. Ira's tragic tale is almost unbelievable so when Ellen must tell about it no one believes her.

Cleaver, Vera
A2
Lady Ellen Grae
Lippincott, 1968

Ellen is sent to live with her aunt so she can learn to be a lady; it is not a completely successful plan. Ellen Grae teaches Laura a few of her less than lady-like ways.

Cleaver, Vera
A3
Grover
Lippincott, 1970

Grover's mother dies and his life changes as he grows up. His friend, Ellen, tries to help as his father can't or won't cope.

Clifford, Eth
1
Help! I'm a Prisoner in the Library
Houghton, 1979

Mary Rose and Jo-Beth go looking for a restroom after their father left them to go look for a gas station. They get locked in the library and are scared when they hear strange noises.

Clifford, Eth
2
Dastardly Murder of Dirty Pete
Houghton, 1981

Again Mary Rose and Jo-Beth are traveling with their father. They get lost looking for grandmother's house. Instead they find the Inn of The Whispering Ghost and an old murder mystery.

Clifford, Eth
3
Just Tell Me When We're Dead
Houghton, 1983

Mary Rose and Jo-Beth are staying with their cousin, Jeff, while their father takes his mother to the hospital. Jeff runs away and while the girls are trying to find him they find a bank robber.

Clifford, Eth
4
Scared Silly
Houghton, 1988

Mary Rose and Jo-Beth go to a shoe museum called "Walk Your Way Around The World." The owner is a magician and when Chinese slippers are found missing the adventure begins.

Clifford, Eth
A1
Harvey's Horrible Snake Disaster
Houghton, 1984

Harvey and his cousin Nora come to terms when she helps him overcome his fear of snakes. She is generally an unlikeable liar but is also creative. She takes a snake home and causes havoc.

Clifford, Eth
A2
Harvey's Marvelous Monkey Mystery
Houghton, 1987

Harvey's cousin Nora is visiting on spring vacation. Strange things begin to happen, like a monkey appearing at night, a mysterious man also appears.

Collier, James
1
Jump Ship to Freedom
Delacorte, 1981

A 14-year-old slave, Daniel, wanting to buy freedom for himself and his mother, escapes from his dishonest master and tries to find help in getting back his continental notes.

Collier, James
2
War Comes to Willy Freeman
Delacorte, 1983

A 13-year-old Black girl, Willy, often mistaken for a boy, loses her father during the Revolutionary War. Her mother disappears and she goes to New York City to find her.

Collier, James
3
Who Is Carrie?
Delacorte, 1984

Carrie observes historic events and at the same time solves the mystery of her own identity. She is a friend of Daniel and a cousin to Willy and finds information important to them all.

Collier, James
A1
Teddy Bear Habit
Norton, 1967

George knows that at 12 he shouldn't depend on his teddy bear but when his father gives it away he tries to recapture it leading to unexpected adventure.

Collier, James
A2
Rich and Famous
Four Winds, 1975

George is now 13 and plays the guitar. A record company makes an offer and George sees himself as a star. But he must contend with agents, TV and advertising people.

Conford, Ellen
1
Dear Lovey Hart,
I Am Desparate
Little, 1975
Carrie and Chip work on the school newspaper and Carrie gets into trouble trying to conceal her identity and the fact that her father is school counselor.

Conford, Ellen
2
We Interrupt This Semester
for an Important Bulletin
Little, 1979
Carrie takes up reporting to impress Chip and only gets into more trouble as she investigates the school cafeteria.

Constant, Alberta
1
Those Miller Girls
Crowell, 1965
Maddy and Lou Emma, along with their professor father make up the Miller family. Reckless, carefree girls with little control have a wild time in the early 1900s.

Constant, Alberta
2
Motoring Millers
Crowell, 1967
Can you picture a car in 1911! Maddy, Lou Emma, their father and his new wife, Kate, take a trip in their new bright red car, named Great Smith. Some discipline has entered the girls' lives.

Constant, Alberta
3
Does Anyone Care
about Lou Emma Miller?
Crowell, 1979
Lou Emma is now 15 and she helps the suffragettes elect the first woman mayor of Gloriosa, Kansas.

Cooper, Margaret
1
Solution: Escape
Walker, 1980
Set in the twenty-first century, Stefan finds out he is a clone and is part of a scheme to control the government. Evonn is his look-alike. They both try to escape. But to where?

Cooper, Margaret
2
Code Name: Clone
Walker, 1982
Evonn and Stefan reach America in 2060 trying to find the "father." They flee capture in the tunnels of New York City. Guard dogs, agents and drugs are all used to try to capture them.

Cooper, Susan
1
Over Sea, Under Stone
Harcourt, 1965
Jane, Barney and Simon find a treasure map leading them to the grail of King Arthur. They are threatened by the Dark but Great-Uncle Merry protects them.

Cooper, Susan
2
Dark Is Rising
Atheneum, 1973
Will, with the help of Great-Uncle Merry must find the six Signs that are necessary to fight off Evil. Will is the seventh son of a seventh son and the last of the Old Ones.

Cooper, Susan
3
Greenwitch
Atheneum, 1974
A legend of the Wild Magic of Earth. The Drew children and Will help the Old Ones recover the grail. They must restore the good power of Greenwitch with the help of Great-Uncle Merry.

Cooper, Susan
4
Grey King
Atheneum, 1975
Will and a white dog with silver eyes must be ready for a dreadful battle with evil. King Arthur's son Bran will help to awaken the Sleepers.

Cooper, Susan
5
Silver on the Trees
Atheneum, 1977
    Will, Bran and the Drew children try to locate the crystal sword which will vanquish the Dark forces. They travel through time and space to see that Light wins out over Evil.

Corbett, Scott
1
Lemonade Trick
Little, 1960
    Kirby and his magical chemistry kit turn lemonade into a drink that makes everyone do good deeds. Kirby cleans the garage and Waldo digs up his bones. The whole town is changed.

Corbett, Scott
2
Mailbox Trick
Little, 1961
    When Kirby's aunt sends him stationery for a birthday present, he doesn't write Thank You notes but starts to send nasty letters to the people in town he doesn't like.

Corbett, Scott
3
Disappearing Dog Trick
Little, 1963
    This time Kirby uses his chemistry kit to find his dog, Waldo, missing after a city campaign to pick up stray dogs.

Corbett, Scott
4
Limerick Trick
Little, 1964
    Kirby wants to win a bicycle by writing the best poem in school. He got started on limericks and found that he could only speak in limericks much to the dismay of his friends and teachers.

Corbett, Scott
5
Baseball Trick
Little, 1965
    Kirby and his magic chemistry set helps the batting of his team but he gets surprising results.

Corbett, Scott
6
Turnabout Trick
Little, 1967
    Kirby and his friends with the aid of the magic chemistry set have more troublesome adventures. A cat doesn't remember he's a cat. Waldo thinks he is a cat. It all comes out okay in the end.

Corbett, Scott
7
Hairy Horror Trick
Little, 1969
    Kirby brings disaster to himself, his friend and his dog, Waldo by misusing his chemistry set. Waldo becomes furless while Kirby and Fenton grow magical hair.

Corbett, Scott
8
Hateful, Plateful Trick
Little, 1971
    Again the chemistry set is the culprit, with Kirby's help. It seems that everyone is surrounded with the smell of the food they hate most.

Corbett, Scott
9
Homerun Trick
Little, 1973
    Should the team really try to win this game if they must then play a GIRLS team? Both teams try very hard to lose!

Corbett, Scott
10
Hockey Trick
Little, 1974
    Kirby and the Panthers resort to a magical hockey puck in a game to save their clubhouse.

Corbett, Scott
11
Black Mask Trick
Little, 1976
    Mrs. Graymalkin, who has talents that are very like a witch, enlists Kirby and his dog Waldo to expose a crook. The crook is one of the town's founders.

Corbett, Scott
12

Hangman's Ghost Trick
Little, 1977

Kirby and his friend look for a special weed that grows in the mountains. They find the weed, and a missing cat, but not before some scarey times.

Corbett, Scott
A1
Case of the Gone Goose
Little, 1966

Inspector Tearle, a young detective, comes across a triple murder—of Geese named Tom, Dick and Harry.

Corbett, Scott
A2
Case of the Fugitive Firebug
Little, 1969

Inspector Tearle's alarm goes off in his tree house office. He finds that someone has set fire to a garage containing an antique car, the Bearcat.

Corbett, Scott
A3
Case of the Ticklish Tooth
Little, 1974

When Inspector Tearle goes to his dentist he finds him bound and gagged. The red-bearded thug escaped on Roger Tearle's bicycle.

Corbett, Scott
A4
Case of the Silver Skull
Little, 1974

Inspector Tearle is asked to watch the silver collection at a Home Tour. Sure enough two antique dealers are there to steal.

Corbett, Scott
A5
Case of the Burgled Blessing Box
Little, 1975

There is money being stolen from the collection box at a Tent Church. It looks like an inside job and Inspector Tearle must solve the robbery.

Corbett, Scott
B1
Tree House Island
Little, 1958

Skip and Harvey come across bank robbers digging up the money they buried 20 years before.

Corbett, Scott
B2
Cutlass Island
Little, 1962

Skip and Harvey, amateur detectives, find old Civil War weapons and a whole arsenal buried on Cutlass Island.

Corbett, W. J.
1
Song of Pentecost
Dutton, 1982

The mice that live on the farm must move or die. Under a courageous leader they flee toward safety. Their leader dies and the mice end their search. Frog's lies endanger Owl's life.

Corbett, W. J.
2
Pentecost, the Chosen One
Delacorte, 1987

A new leader emerges. He is the son of the last great leader but feels inadequate. Deep friendships develop as he leads his followers toward their destiny.

Corcoran, Barbara
1
You're Allegro Dead
Atheneum, 1981

Two girls discover a mystery at their recently reopened summer camp. Was someone living there while it was closed? A bank robber hid his loot in the pond.

Corcoran, Barbara
2
Watery Grave
Atheneum, 1982

Kim and Stella work to find the killer when a swimming pool murder occurs in a household they are visiting. Drugs seem to be involved.

Corcoran, Barbara
3
August, Die She Must
Atheneum, 1984

A feud over the merits of two counselors divides the campers at

Camp Allegro until one of the counselors is found dead.

Corcoran, Barbara
4
Mystery on Ice
Atheneum, 1985
   A series of mysterious threats escalate into dangerous and frightening events. Kim and Stella face men and dogs who see them as intruders. The camp is to be sold and buildings set afire.

Cormier, Robert
1
Chocolate War
Patheon, 1974
   Jerry refuses to sell chocolates for a private school fund-raiser and is harassed by the school bully, Archie. The student body is at the mercy of Archie and his "tricks."

Cormier, Robert
2
Beyond the Chocolate War
Knopf, 1985
   Dark deeds continue at Trinity High School, ending in a public demonstration of a homemade guillotine. There is a good deal of human unkindness in and around school.

Craven, Margaret
1
I Heard the Owl Call My Name
Doubleday, 1973
   A moving story of a man's discovery of truth as he works among the Northwest Indians.

Craven, Margaret
2
Again Call the Owl
Putnam, 1980
   How the dying minister, who won the respect and friendship of the Kwakiutl Indians of the Northwest, faces death.

Cresswell, Helen
1
Ordinary Jack
Macmillan, 1977
   Jack is the only ordinary boy of the talented and eccentric Bagthorpe fam-ily. He concocts a scheme to distinguish himself as a prophet with ESP.

Cresswell, Helen
2
Absolute Zero
Macmillan, 1978
   Members of the talented and eccentric Bagthorpe family channel their energies into slogan writing contests and taking labels off cans of food. Zero, the pet dog, can't sniff dog bones.

Cresswell, Helen
3
Bagthorpes Unlimited
Macmillan, 1978
   The competitive Bagthorpes join forces in a rare display of solidarity when Grandma organizes a family reunion. They plan zany incidents to annoy the rest of the relatives.

Cresswell, Helen
4
Bagthorpes vs. the World
Macmillan, 1979
   The Bagthorpes contend with father's attempts to be self-sufficient. Because he mistakenly thinks they are poor, he wants them to raise their own food and keep animals.

Cresswell, Helen
5
Bagthorpes Abroad
Macmillan, 1984
   This time the Bagthorpes are on vacation in Wales, but in a haunted house where they want to learn more about ghosts. One incident after another happen to make life chaotic.

Cresswell, Helen
6
Bagthorpes Haunted
Macmillan, 1985
   Still on vacation in the haunted house, the Bagthorpes try to contact the ghosts living there.

Cunningham, Julia
1
Burnish Me Bright
Pantheon, 1970

Auguste is a mute orphan. He is victimized by his fellow villagers. A brutal story with a valuable message. An old mime befriends him and teaches him his craft.

Cunningham, Julia
2
Far in the Day
Pantheon, 1972

Auguste wanders through Europe as a circus performer in search of food, warmth, friendship and a HOME.

Cunningham, Julia
3
Silent Voice
Dutton, 1981

Auguste is found by street urchin and is befriended by a famous Parisian mime, Ms. Bernard. But jealousy of his talent hinders his life, especially by the backer of the school.

Cunningham, Julia
A1
Onion Journey
Pantheon, 1967

Although written later, this story is about Gilly when he lives with his grandmother before the orphanage.

Cunningham, Julia
A2
Dorp Dead
Knopf, 1965

Gilly is in an orphanage and sent away to live with a carpenter. He is unhappy and misused. So he escapes.

Curry, Jane
1
Wolves of Aam
Atheneum, 1981

Runner, the fastest Tiddi (little folk) scout, is befriended by Lek. He goes to the stark fortress of Gzel in the mountains of Icelands to find his special stone and its meaning.

Curry, Jane
2
Shadow Dancers
Atheneum, 1983

Wrongfully accused of stealing a valuable moonstone Lek enters the dread Shadowland to look for stones of equal power.

Curry, Jane
A1
Parsley, Sage, Rosemary and Time
Harcourt, 1975

Parsley Sage is the cat. Rosemary is the girl and Time (thyme) is on the stone which takes Rosemary back to the time of the Pilgrims. She is put in jail with Goody Cakebread, a witch.

Curry, Jane
A2
Magical Cupboard
Atheneum, 1976

A preacher steals a cupboard from a widow who he says is a witch. He takes it to an orphanage and Felicity discovers its magic. Felicity and Rosemary are connected through time by this magic.

Curry, Jane
B1
Beneath the Hill
Harcourt, 1967

Miggie planned a treasure hunt but someone else was interested in her treasures and her carefully planted clues. She found the door leading to Kaolin and his strange family.

Curry, Jane
B2
Daybreakers
Harcourt, 1970

Callie, Liss and Harry stumbled upon an underground cave. They were transported back to the time of an earlier Indian civilization. They were captured and jailed but later rescued.

Curry, Jane
B3
Birdstone
Atheneum, 1977

A girl is created by Callie and her friends to fight boredom. The real girl shows up from the time of the Abaloc Indians. She is looking for her grandfather who has been lost for 1600 years.

Curry, Jane
C1

Mindy's Mysterious Miniature
Atheneum, 1970

A young girl finds an old dollhouse with magical powers no one knew about.

Curry, Jane
C2
The Lost Farm
Atheneum, 1974

The farm and everything on it is reduced to miniature by a mysterious machine. Pete and his grandmother do all they can to keep from being lost forever.

D'ignazio, Fred
1
Chip Mitchell, Case of the Stolen Computer Brains
Dutton, 1982

A seventh grade computer whiz solves ten puzzling cases using his knowledge of logic and computers.

D'ignazio, Fred
2
Chip Mitchell, Case of the Robot Warriors
Dutton, 1984

The reader helps Chip solve these eight puzzling mysteries with the use of logic and clear thinking. Sherwin, the robot and Hermes, the computer help.

Dahl, Roald
1
Charlie and the Chocolate Factory
Knopf, 1964

Each of the five winners of the Willy Wonka contest is put to a test as they visit the chocolate factory. The tour seems to bring out the best and the worst of the visitors.

Dahl, Roald
2
Charlie and the Great Glass Elevator
Hall, 1972

Charlie, his family and Mr. Wonka are launched into space by the great glass elevator. The President tries to untangle the mess but makes it worse. In the end Willie saves the Earth.

Dank, Milton
1
Dangerous Game
Lippincott, 1977

Charles matures quickly while serving the French Resistance during World War II. He meets with French traitors and German Nazis.

Dank, Milton
2
Game's End
Lippincott, 1979

Charles, now 19, is an officer in the Free French Army. He is also a spy for the English in France as the Allies prepare for invasion.

Dank, Milton
A1
Computer Caper
Delacorte, 1983

Attempting to help friends, the Galaxy Gang battles money swindlers. They use computer expertise and psychology to capture the crooks.

Dank, Milton
A2
U.F.O. Has Landed
Delacorte, 1983

Glowing green lights and strange creatures from outer space land on Earth and a teacher sees it. He is to be fired unless the Galaxy Gang can prove its existence.

Dank, Milton
A3
3-D Traitors
Delacorte, 1984

The ghost of Benedict Arnold is seen in the old house of a friend who is being pressured into selling the house. The Galaxy Gang find that the ghost is created by a hologram.

Dank, Milton
A4
Treasure Code
Delacorte, 1985

The treasure is a dragon ring, and the clues are hidden in a book by a local author. The Galaxy Gang looks everywhere in the city. The clues involve geography, history, math, music, etc.

Dank, Milton
A5
Computer Game Murder
Delacorte, 1985

Mr. "Chips" and "Peter Pan" are playing a computer game when "I'm scared. Help me." shows up on the screen. It is another case for the Galaxy Gang.

Dank, Milton
B1
Khaki Wings
Delacorte, 1980

Edward, 16, joins the Royal Flying Corps. He is the only survivor of his original squadron and finds that war is not romantic but cruel and terrifying.

Dank, Milton
B2
Red Flight Two
Delacorte, 1981

Edward finds action in the Royal Flying Corps during World War II. His best friend is killed and he is made Flight Instructor. But he wants to use his experience and so heads a squadron.

Danziger, Paula
1
Cat Ate My Gymsuit
Delacorte, 1974

Marcy, a very courageous and imaginative girl, is bored with school and herself until Ms. Finney comes to teach English. Independent stands and moral values are at stake.

Danziger, Paula
2
There's a Bat in Bunk Five
Delacorte, 1980

Marcy is now a camp counselor and realizes what a heavy responsibility that is. She is also faced with some new boy-girl experiences.

De Clements, Barthe
1
Nothing's Fair in the Fifth Grade
Viking, 1981

Elsie is new in school; she is fat and unhappy about it. She is accused of stealing money for candy but Jenny,

one of the "in" girls helps Elsie through friendship and understanding.

De Clements, Barthe
2
6th Grade Can Really Kill You
Viking, 1985

Elsie's friend Helen is a pest in school and her grades are not good but she is a star baseball pitcher and has a sense of humor. A new teacher helps Helen straighten out her problems.

De Clements, Barthe
3
How Do You Lose
Those 9th Grade Blues?
Delacorte, 1983

Elsie starts high school and finds the best looking boy on the Team showing interest in her. She lost her fat and is cute but she still thinks FAT. She is jealous and distrustful of Craddac.

De Clements, Barthe
4
Seventeen and In-Between
Viking, 1984

Elsie, in the beginning was fat, became slim and attractive but was insecure because of her own thoughts. Now she has not only a boyfriend but boyfriend problems she never dreamed of.

Deleon, Eric
1
Pitch and Hasty Check It Out
Orchard, 1988

Pitch and Hasty are hiding out at Harrington's Mall looking for what makes a strange noise back of the pinball machine. They find parrot smugglers and are accidentally flown miles from home.

Delton, Judy
Pr1
Kitty from the Start

Kitty moves to a new house and must make adjustments to her new life. Everything is different from what she has known. Kitty is nine years old and just meets Mary and Eillen.

Delton, Judy
1

Kitty in the Middle
Houghton, 1979
   Three friends from school have a good time growing up in the early '40s. They crash a wedding and explore a haunted house, they learn about friendship and love, and have a great deal of fun.

Delton, Judy
2
Kitty in the Summer
Houghton, 1980
   Kitty "purchases" a pagan baby and is exposed to real poverty. She and her two friends have an exciting summer with the baby's African family.

Delton, Judy
3
Kitty in High School
Houghton, 1984
   Kitty, now a Freshman in high school, makes friends, uses make-up and meets some boys to make school life more interesting. There are popular songs, current fads and fashionable clothes.

Delton, Judy
A1
Backyard Angel
Houghton, 1983
   Rags, Angel's younger brother, is a real pain to take care of even though she actually likes him. Mom is working and Angel is on her own since no kids her age live on the block.

Delton, Judy
A2
Angel in Charge
Houghton, 1985
   Mom goes on vacation leaving Angel and Rags in care of Alyce who goes to the hospital and leaves them alone.

Delton, Judy
A3
Angel's Mother's Boyfriend
Houghton, 1986
   What is Angel to think when she finds out her mother's boyfriend is a clown? Rudy lives in Washington, D.C. and Angel thinks the letters from him are from the IRA. She tries to help.

Delton, Judy
A4
Angel's Mother's Wedding
Houghton, 1987
   Angel is worried about her mother's plans for the wedding. Will it really happen and on time! What about flowers? Gifts? Angel also realizes that being adopted means more than a name change.

Dickinson, Peter
1
Weathermonger
Little, 1969
[Later in time than #2 Heartsease.]
   Geoffrey and Sally, sentenced to death by drowning because they were witches, escape. They return to learn more about the Changes. Anyone found with a machine of any kind was put to death.

Dickinson, Peter
2
Heartsease
Little, 1969
   "Changes" made people hate machinery. Maragret and Jonathan find an American engineer, stoned for being a witch. They help him escape to Heartsease, a tug boat.

Dickinson, Peter
3
Devil's Children
Little, 1970
   Nicky is alone, separated from her parents, and finds that she is the only one who can be the link between the Sikhs, the outcasts, and the villagers who are affected by the Changes.

Dicks, Terrance
1
Case of the Missing Masterpiece
Lodestar, 1978
   The Baker Street Irregulars are young detectives who solve neighborhood crimes and when a painting is stolen from a valuable art collection they must begin their work.

Dicks, Terrance
2

Case of the Blackmail Boys
Lodestar, 1979
A bank robbery plot is discovered and foiled by the clouthing Baker Street Irregulars. They discover blackmail is being used to get inside information.

Dicks, Terrance
3
Case of the Cinema Swindle
Lodestar, 1980
The Irregulars investigate the burning of the local theater. It is suspected of being arson.

Dicks, Terrance
4
Case of the Crooked Kids
Lodestar, 1978
The Baker Street Irregulars must stop other youngsters, who are being led by crooked adults, from getting into the stealing racket.

Dicks, Terrance
5
Case of the Ghost Grabbers
Lodestar, 1980
A ghost haunts the home of Sir Jasper (from Missing Masterpiece) and the investigation leads to the far past. Dan is injured and helps solve the mystery from his hospital bed.

Dicks, Terrance
6
Case of the Cop Catchers
Lodestar, 1981
The Irregulars have difficulty solving a whole series of strange happenings involving their friend Detective Day, who disappears. Truck hijacking and jewel thefts are among them.

Divine, David
1
Stolen Season
Crowell, 1967
Clint, Peter and Mig make a bet and their gambling leads to a breathtaking adventure.

Divine, David
2
Three Red Flares
Crowell, 1972
Mig, Peter and Clint have another adventure; this time a map starts the search.

Dixon, Paige
1
May I Cross Your Golden River
Atheneum, 1975
Jordan is 18 when he notices the first sign of his terminal illness. Skipper, his young brother, and the rest of his family have a hard time accepting Jordan's fate.

Dixon, Paige
2
Skipper
Atheneum, 1979
Jordan is dead but Skipper has not made a satisfying adjustment. He doesn't understand the why's and wherefore's of life and death.

Donaldson, Margaret
1
Journey into War
André Deutsch, 1979
Two boys and a girl help to fight the Germans in London during World War II. In this story the girl gets caught and needs to be rescued.

Donaldson, Margaret
2
Moon's on Fire
André Deutsch, 1980
Janey and the refugee twins are in the London blitz. They stay with reluctant relatives, and find both enemies and strange allies along the docks. Uncle Maurice hunts spies.

Doty, Jean
1
Summer Pony
Macmillan, 1973
Mokey, a pony, is the central character of Ginny's greatest summer experience. She cares for this run-down pony and she becomes hers.

Doty, Jean
2
Winter Pony
Macmillan, 1975

Ginny owns Mokey and trains her to pull a sleigh. Mokey gives birth to a foal.

Du Jardin, Rosamond
1
Practically Seventeen
Lippicott, 1949

The story of Toby with all the troubles and joys of living with sisters who give advice about all Toby should know as she grows up, especially boys.

Du Jardin, Rosamond
2
Class Ring
Lippincott, 1951

Toby is 17 and wears Brose's class ring and is going "steady." Her parents are against it. She is also getting the attention of a college boy, Dick.

Du Jardin, Rosamond
3
Boy Trouble
Lippincott, 1953

This is Toby's last summer before going to college. She has a summer job and learns more about life and especially boys.

Du Jardin, Rosamond
4
Real Thing
Lippincott, 1956

Now that Toby is in college she has conflicting thoughts about her high school romance with Brose.

Du Jardin, Rosamond
5
Wedding in the Family
Lippincott, 1958

This is the introduction of Midge, Toby's younger sister, who now stars as Toby gets married.

Du Jardin, Rosamond
6
One of the Crowd
Lippincott, 1961

This is still a Toby sequel but it is more about her younger sister, Midge. Midge is a high school sophomore and faces the dilemma of "good old friends" and "smart new ones."

Du Jardin, Rosamond
A1
Double Date
Lippincott, 1952

Pam and Penny face the problems, situations and happenings of all girls growing up. But being a twin adds to these problems, especially when they are so different temperamentally.

Du Jardin, Rosamond
A2
Double Feature
Lippincott, 1953

Pam and Penny are now in their first year of college. Being "grown up" does not ease problems with their family or with their relationships with boys.

Du Jardin, Rosamond
A3
Showboat Summer
Lippincott, 1955

Pam and Penny have finished one year of college and are ready for a vacation and choose a trip on a river boat.

Du Jardin, Rosamond
A4
Double Wedding
Lippincott, 1959

Pam and Penny are getting married but both their fiancés want to wait to graduate first and this causes some real problems.

Du Jardin, Rosamond
B1
Wait for Marcy
Lippincott, 1950

Marcy is 15 and is having her first real date. She learns about dating and growing up. But she and Steve quarrel. Marcy's older brother is the source of the problems.

Du Jardin, Rosamond
B2
Marcy Catches Up
Lippincott, 1952

Marcy spends a summer on a Colorado ranch where she has a wonderful romantic adventure and does some growing up.

Du Jardin, Rosamond
B3
Man for Marcy
Lippincott, 1954

Marcy's boyfriend, Steve, is away at college and this leaves Marcy without an escort to any social events. She needs to do something about this.

Du Jardin, Rosamond
B4
Senior Prom
Lippincott, 1957

This is Marcy's last year in high school. She is excited about graduation. There are boy and date problems. First two and then no date for that all-important Senior Prom.

Duane, Diane
1
So You Want to Be a Wizard
Delacorte, 1983

Bullied because she won't fight back, Nita looks for assistance in a book of wizardry and gets results. Her friend, Kit, has the same book: "Book of Night with Moon."

Duane, Diane
2
Deep Wizardry
Delacorte, 1985

During the summer vacation, Nita the wizard, helps Sreee combat an evil power.

Dunnahoo, Terry
1
Who Cares About Espie Sanchez?
Dutton, 1975

Espie was a loner, running from a bad home. But, faced with juvenile hall, or facing Mrs. Garcia, Espie made her tough decision.

Dunnahoo, Terry
2
This Is Espie Sanchez
Dutton, 1976

After being arrested for running away from home, Espie now works for the police as an Explorer Scout. But, smuggling and murder is still ahead when Teresa is brought in, very troubled.

Dunnahoo, Terry
3
Who Needs Espie Sanchez?
Dutton, 1975

Alcoholism is now a problem in Espie's life. Her curiosity is aroused by a young girl who befriends her after both are in an accident.

Eager, Edward
1
Half Magic
Harcourt, 1954

The children must spend the summer in a city apartment and need to pass the time. They find fantastic adventure by double-wishing on an ancient coin.

Eager, Edward
2
Knight's Castle
Harcourt, 1956

Jane, Katharine, Mark and Martha re-enact the writings of Scott with great success.

Eager, Edward
3
Magic by the Lake
Harcourt, 1957

A turtle tells the four children about the magic lake. Their wishes were probably poorly made and they find themselves in more danger than delight.

Eager, Edward
4
Time Garden
Harcourt, 1958

By rubbing bits of thyme and wishing, the Natterjack (a frog) allows the four children to be transported through time: a ride with the Minute Men, a visit to the Alcotts and a Queen.

Eager, Edward
A1
Magic or Not?
Harcourt, 1959

In this books we meet Gordy, Lydia, Laura and Kip. We also learn of the magic wishing well the children discover that autumn.

Eager, Edward
A2
Well-Wishers
Harcourt, 1960
There is magic in the old wishing well. Each child has his own wish fulfilled while all of them participate, Gordy, Laura, Kip, and Lydia. Each wish is well carried out.

Ellison, Lucile
1
Butter on Both Sides
Scribner's, 1979
Lucy plans an overnight trip up the Tombigbee River. Her father gets seriously ill and Christmas must be delayed until the Fourth of July when he is well and the family is reunited.

Ellison, Lucile
2
Tie That Binds
Scribner's, 1981
Lucy helps put out a tragic fire in which her mother's quilts are used to smother the flames. She must also cope with a new baby in the family and a sister who dies.

Elmore, Patricia
1
Susannah and the Blue House Mystery
Dutton, 1980
Susannah and her friend Lucy are "detectives." They search the Blue House for clues and find a missing will. They also discover that someone else is searching the house. The rightful heir wins.

Elmore, Patricia
2
Susannah and the Poison Green Halloween
Dutton, 1982
Someone put poisoned candy in the Trick or Treat bag and Knievel Jones and Carla Abe ate some. Susannah and Lucy must find out who did it.

Emery, Anne
1
Dinny Gordon, Freshman
Macrea, 1959

Dinny is not interested in boys as are her friends. But she gets involved with a senior, Clyde. Her best friend dates Clyde when Dinny gets the measles. She wants to go to Rome to study.

Emery, Anne
2
Dinny Gordon, Sophomore
Macrae, 1961
Curt breaks up with Sue, Dinny's best friend, and takes an interest in Dinny.

Emery, Anne
3
Dinny Gordon, Junior
Macrae, 1964
After a break-up and reconciliation, Dinny discovers that her boyfriend, Curt, has strong prejudices against some of her Jewish friends.

Emery, Anne
4
Dinny Gordon, Senior
Macrae, 1967
Dinny is now a senior. Her views of friendship and boyfriends have changed from the experiences of the last few years. She goes on to a satisfying future.

Engdahl, Sylvia
1
This Star Shall Abide
Atheneum, 1972
A future world where machines are not built but "just are." However, this planet's metal is unsuitable for machinery. Noren questions the holders of power and is punished.

Engdahl, Sylvia
2
Beyond Tomorrow Mountain
Atheneum, 1973
Noren's planet is destined for disaster until he learns to accept a promise and hope. He becomes a Scholar and goes to build a city on the other side of Tomorrow Mountain.

Engdahl, Sylvia
3
Doors of the Universe
Atheneum, 1981
Noren, now an adult, does not have

all the knowledge he needs to solve his problems. His wife, Talyra, dies and he studies even more until he can find a way to help people.

Engdahl, Sylvia
A1
Enchantress from the Stars
Atheneum, 1970
Elana arrives on Andrecia by chance and Georyn believes she is there to save Andrecia from the dragons. She must not reveal herself or use any of her powers, but must work as best she can.

Engdahl, Sylvia
A2
Far Side of Evil
Atheneum, 1971
Elana was sent to Toris, a planet in the Critical Stage, to help in the reconstruction after a disaster, but meets with jail, torture and possible death.

Enright, Elizabeth
1
Saturdays
Holt, 1941
Each Saturday one of the children picks a favorite activity, and then is allowed to pursue it with the pooled allowance of all the children.

Enright, Elizabeth
2
Four Story Mistake
Holt, 1942
The Melendy family move to the country, into a house that is a BIG MISTAKE. But each of the children find something special: a running brook, an orchard, a cave and a cellar.

Enright, Elizabeth
3
Then There Were Five
Holt, 1944
The Melendy children are on their own, and get involved in some wild adventures: Mona in her first attempt at baking and cooking, a confrontation with the DeLacey's and the Red Cross.

Enright, Elizabeth
4

Spiderweb for Two
Holt, 1951
Two older children are away at school and the two that are left at home, Randy and Oliver, find new adventures, while waiting for the holidays when everyone will be home.

Enright, Elizabeth
A1
Goneaway Lake
Harcourt, 1957
Portia and her cousin Julian discover abandoned cottages near a swamp that once was a lake. An old man lives in one and his sister in another. They relive the past when the lake was there.

Enright, Elizabeth
A2
Return to Goneaway Lake
Harcourt, 1961
Portia's family is going to buy and restore the old cottages then live there year round. Portia is delighted!

Erdman, Louisa
1
Wind Blows Free
Dodd, 1952
Melindy Pierce moves to the Panhandle in Texas and misses her old friends. She makes a new friend, David, and learns to like her new home.

Erdman, Louisa
2
Wide Horizon
Dodd, 1956
Shy and timid Katie Pierce is 15 and lives in Texas. She has to learn responsibility early in life.

Estes, Eleanor
1
Ginger Pye
Harcourt, 1951
A very smart puppy named Ginger is missing for months before the mystery is solved. Three-year-old Uncle Bennie helps in the return of this puppy bought by Jerry and Rachel.

Estes, Eleanor
2

Pinky Pye
Harcourt, 1958

Pinky, a black kitten, boxes with Ginger, uses the typewriter and does many other funny things. She was acquired on Fire Island while the Pye family was on vacation to study birds.

Estes, Eleanor
A1
Moffats
Harcourt, 1941

A humorous book about a fun-loving, lively family. Each chapter is a different and funny story about Jane, Joey, Rufus and Sylvie.

Estes, Eleanor
A2
Middle Moffat
Harcourt, 1942

Jane is the next to youngest Moffat. This is her story, with her best friend and it is as funny as the Moffats.

Estes, Eleanor
A3
Rufus M
Harcourt, 1943

Rufus, the youngest, is the hero in this story of the Moffat family. He must learn to write his name if he is to get a much wanted library card.

Estes, Eleanor
A4
Moffat Museum
Harcourt, 1983

Jane Moffat opens a museum in the place with which the Moffats are most identified: Cranbury, Conn. Sylvie is married; Rufus dresses up for the wax statues in the museum; Joey is 16.

Estes, Eleanor
B1
Alley
Harcourt, 1964

The Alley is on a college campus and consists of 26 families. A burglary takes place and the Alley's 33 children help in the arrest.

Estes, Eleanor
B2

Tunnel of Hugsy Goode
Harcourt, 1972

Hugsy said there was a tunnel under the Alley and so they search for it. And discover it is there!

Ewing, Kathryn
1
Private Matter
Harcourt, 1975

Marcy, who has no father, thinks of her neighbor Mr. Endicott as a father. When he moves she is hurt and lonely. Then her mother announces that she is getting married again.

Ewing, Kathryn
2
Things Won't Be the Same
Harcourt, 1980

Marcy is startled about her mother's decision to get married. After the wedding Marcy goes to stay with her unknown father. She is again hurt and lonely.

Farley, Walter
1
Black Stallion
Random, 1944

A fabulous horse, Black, and a boy, Alec, share a desert island when both are shipwrecked. They are rescued and Alec trains the horse to race.

Farley, Walter
2
Black Stallion Returns
Random, 1945

Black is taken by his rightful owners. Alec accompanies two men to Arabia in search of the missing Black Stallion. He rides him in an Arabian race.

Farley, Walter
3
Son of Black Stallion
Random, 1947

Satan, Black's son, comes back with Alec. He realizes that this desert born stallion cannot be entirely free of his natural instinct to kill when he begins to tame and train him.

Farley, Walter
4

Black Stallion and Satan
Random, 1949
   Which is the fastest racer—Black Stallion or his son, Satan? It will be determined when Black comes to America to race.

Farley, Walter
5
Black Stallion's Blood Bay Colt
Random, 1950
   Black Stallion's second son, Bonfire, likes harness racing. He must be tamed, trained and well handled.

Farley, Walter
6
Black Stallion's Filly
Random, 1952
   The Black Stallion's filly is trained by Alec and Henry to win the Kentucky Derby. But, she has a strong will, and the training is complicated. Can she make it to the great Classic?

Farley, Walter
7
Black Stallion Revolts
Random, 1953
   The Black Stallion breaks free and lives the wild life he was destined to live.

Farley, Walter
8
Black Stallion's Sulky Colt
Random, 1954
   Bonfire, one of Black's sons, has problems learning to race in harness (Sulky) but because of some accidents which frightened the colt, Alec must try harness racing.

Farley, Walter
9
Black Stallion's Courage
Random, 1956
   The Black Stallion runs in the race of the century.

Farley, Walter
10
Black Stallion Mystery
Random, 1957
   Where did the three black colts come from? They are not the Black's.

Farley, Walter
11
Black Stallion and Flame
Random, 1960
   Stranded on an island after a plane wreck the Black Stallion meets a filly named Flame.

Farley, Walter
12
Black Stallion Challenged
Random, 1964
   The Black Stallion is challenged to a race by Flame and Flame can really run.

Farley, Walter
13
Black Stallion's Ghost
Random, 1969
   Alec was knocked out by Captain and Black flees into the Everglades. It was his most terrifying day, and night. Alec ends up buying the white Ghost horse from this circus captain.

Farley, Walter
14
Black Stallion and the Girl
Random, 1971
   Alec meets and hires a girl, Pam, who trains horses. Henry doesn't like it. When Alec is suspended she rides the horse and proves her courage.

Farley, Walter
15
Black Stallion Legend
Random, 1983
   Alec and Black travel to the Southwest and help an Indian tribe after an earthquake thereby fulfilling an ancient prophecy.

Farley, Walter
A1
Island Stallion
Random, 1948
   Steve saves Flame from a horrible death and a friendship begins, one that would change both their lives.

Farley, Walter
A2
Island Stallion's Fury
Random, 1951

Some very dangerous men find the secret valley of the stallion. Steve is very concerned about this. It could mean trouble.

Farley, Walter
A3
Island Stallion Races
Random, 1955

An untrained stallion on a racetrack makes for a very thrilling story. Can Flame run in competition?

Farmer, Penelope
1
Summer Birds
Harcourt, 1962

A strange boy teaches Charlotte and Emma to fly. He takes them on a moonlit flight to a lake and to a sea. When summer is over he leaves.

Farmer, Penelope
2
Emma in Winter
Harcourt, 1966

Charlotte goes to boarding school and Emma is alone. She makes friends with one of her classmates, Bobby, and tells him of her summer spent flying with the strange boy.

Farmer, Penelope
3
Charlotte Sometimes
Harcourt, 1969

Charlotte slips back in time and becomes another girl, Clare Moby. She moves back and forth and although she wants to stay in the present she does not want to lose her friend from the past.

Fitzgerald, John
1
Great Brain
Dial, 1967

A funny story about a "brainy" boy and his friends. He outwits adults and hatches great money-making schemes.

Fitzgerald, John
2
More Adventures of the Great Brain
Dial, 1969

Tom (Great Brain) is at it again with more antics. He even astounds the adults around him.

Fitzgerald, John
3
Me and My Little Brain
Dial, 1971

Tom's younger brother is ready to try all his brother's tricks. He does not have the same success but does trap a criminal and saves a small child.

Fitzgerald, John
4
Great Brain at the Academy
Dial, 1972

Another story about Tom and his brother at the Catholic Academy for Boys.

Fitzgerald, John
5
Great Brain Reforms
Dial, 1973

The Great Brain tries to reform because his friends hold a mock trial and threaten to make him an outcast.

Fitzgerald, John
6
Return of the Great Brain
Dial, 1974

More outrageous schemes of the Great Brain, who can't keep his promise to reform. He does get involved in solving a crime.

Fitzgerald, John
7
Great Brain Does It Again
Dial, 1975

J.D. tells more about the great brain of Tom and how he can get out of any situation, no matter how bizarre. Earning money is still the main concern.

Fitzhugh, Louise
1
Harriet the Spy
Harper, 1964

Harriet wants to be a writer. She "observes" her friends and neighbors, keeping a notebook. This notebook gets her into a great deal of trouble.

Fitzhugh, Louise
2
Long Secret
Harper, 1965

This book includes Beth Ellen, Harriet's best friend. As both girls begin to grow up, they begin to understand friendship. They investigate the notes being left everywhere.

Fitzhugh, Louise
3
Sport
Delacorte, 1979

Sport is Harriet's friend. When he inherits millions of dollars his mother wants the money even though he has lived with his father not her. His friends attempt to rescue him.

Forester, Cecil
1
Mr. Hornblower Midshipman
Little, 1950

The story of how the future Captain, Commodore and Lord started as a midshipman, then became lieutenant in Her Majesty's Navy.

Forester, Cecil
2
Lieutenant Hornblower
Little, 1952

This continues Hornblower's career as a lieutenant and the rivalry with Napoleon. He goes on to become Commander and meets Napoleon head on.

Forester, Cecil
3
Hornblower and the Hotspur
Little, 1962

Commander Hornblower is in a final encounter with Spanish ships laden with treasures for Napoleon. He is in command of the "Hotspur."

Forester, Cecil
4
Hornblower and the Atropos
Little, 1953

The episodes in the early life of Captain Hornblower.

Forester, Cecil
5, 6, 7

Captain Horatio Hornblower
Little, 1939

Contains: "Beat to Quarters," "Ship of the Line" and "Flying Colours." Stories of wooden sailing ships, Napoleonic battles, England's rule of the seas and America's courageous sailors.

Forester, Cecil
8
Commodore Hornblower
Little, 1945

Hornblower challenges Napoleon in the Baltic Sea with his squadron. He must maintain the friendship of Russia and Sweden.

Forester, Cecil
9
Lord Hornblower
Little, 1946

Hornblower is engaged in a great sea battle. Le Havre is captured and he narrowly escapes death.

Forester, Cecil
10
*Admiral Hornblower
in the West Indies*
Little, 1958

In charge of the West Indies Station, Admiral Hornblower guards the French Empire against all comers.

Forester, Cecil
11
Hornblower During Crisis
Little, 1967

Another encounter between Hornblower and Napoleon.

Fyson, Jenny
1
Three Brothers of Ur
Coward, 1964

This story, set 4,000 years ago, tells of trouble and mischief that seems to follow the three sons of a wealthy man. Especially Haran, the youngest as he breaks a religious image.

Fyson, Jenny
2
Journey of the Eldest Son
Coward, 1965

More exciting and unusual adventures of the three brothers. Shamashazer, the eldest, goes on a trading journey and is injured. He is rescued by shepherds.

Garden, Nancy
1
Four Crossings
Farrar, 1981
Jed and Melissa face a menacing old hermit, a golden colored dog, a missing silver plate and an ancient ritual.

Garden, Nancy
2
Watermeet
Farrar, 1983
The crazed old hermit, after kidnapping Jed and Melissa helps to explain the connection between the dog and the plate. It is a combination of legend and witchcraft.

Garfield, Leon
1
Strange Affair of Adelaide Harris
Pantheon, 1971
Harris and Bostock decide to recreate an ancient incident by kidnapping Harris' sister and leaving her to survive alone. But, it all turns out to be a comedy of errors.

Garfield, Leon
2
Night of the Comet
Delacorte, 1979
Harris offers Bostock the affection of his sister in exchange for a valuable brass telescope through which he can observe a Pigott's comet. Another comedy of errors.

Garner, Alan
1
Stone Book
Collins, 1976
Mary wants to learn to read. Her father takes her to a cave that is visited once each generation. It gives Mary a feeling of the continuity of the family.

Garner, Alan
2

Granny Reardon
Collins, 1977
Joseph was raised by his grandparents. He wanted to plan his future different from what was expected of him: that he be a stonemason like his grandfather.

Garner, Alan
3
Aimer Gate
Collins, 1979
Joseph's son Robert is the main character in this third generation family story. He wants to be a soldier like his Uncle Charlie but learns that fighting is dangerous and stark.

Garner, Alan
4
Tom Fobble's Day
Collins, 1979
William, Joseph's grandson, is the forth generation which began with Joseph's grandfather, the stonemason.

Garner, Alan
A1
The Moon of Gomrath
Walck, 1967
Wizard Cadellin sees Old Magic danger coming. Colin and Susan accidentally release the figures of the Wild Hunt and add to the strength of Old Magic.

Garner, Alan
A2
Weirdstone of Brisingamen
Walck, 1969
Colin, Susan, the Wizard Cadellin and others seek to keep Firefrost from evil.

Giff, Patricia
1
Fourth Grade Celebrity
Delacorte, 1979
Cassandra (Casey) tries to find ways to become a well-known girl in school. She runs for class president. Walt will help if she takes Tracy (the pen pal) off his hands.

Giff, Patricia
2

Girl Who Knew It All
Delacorte, 1979

Tracy, whose reading ability is below grade level, tries to hide this fact by strange behavior. How surprising when her pen pal, Casey, comes to visit her.

Giff, Patricia
3
Left-Handed Shortstop
Delacorte, 1980

Walter is not an athlete; he doesn't want to play ball. Casey makes him a phony cast so he can't play and reveal the truth about his playing ability.

Giff, Patricia
4
Winter Worm Business
Delacorte, 1983

Leroy predicts trouble and frustration when his cousin Mitchell moves into the neighborhood. Especially when he tries to cut in on Leroy and Tracy's worm business.

Giff, Patricia
5
Love, from the Fifth Grade Celebrity
Delacorte, 1986

The friendship that started between Tracy and Casey during the summer is running into trouble because of Tracy's popularity when school begins.

Giff, Patricia
A1
Have You Seen Hyacinth Macaw?
Delacorte, 1981

Abby and Potsie are practicing sleuths. When Abby's brother acts unusually strange they stumble upon a theft and a missing person.

Giff, Patricia
A2
Loretta P. Sweeny, Where Are You?
Delacorte, 1983

Abby is at it again. This time a murder is involved and when Abby sees the purple and orange wallet she "knows" it belongs to the murderer. Super, the dog, and a fortune teller are involved.

Giff, Patricia
A3
Tootsie Tanner, Why Don't You Talk?
Delacorte, 1987

Abby Jones sees her neighbor as a suspect in a runaway, and possibly, in a spy case. She jumps to wrong conclusions and misses the right clues. She is looking for a stolen roll of film.

Gilson, Jamie
1
Harvey, the Beer Can King
Lothrop, 1978

Harvey is a collector, he is going to have the largest collection of beer cans in town. He knows he will win the contest but he doesn't count on some misadventurous trading.

Gilson, Jamie
2
Hello, My Name Is Scrambled Eggs
Lothrop, 1984

Harvey, the school's best known student (for a number of different reasons) meets Tuan from Vietnam. His job? Make an American out of him!

Gilson, Jamie
A1
13 Ways to Sink a Sub
Lothrop, 1982

Hobie and his friends think of a contest that will make the substitute teacher cry. Girls team up against boys to see who can make her leave. They try everything imaginable.

Gilson, Jamie
A2
4B Goes Wild
Lothrop, 1983

The class is at Camp Trotter and faces a lot of new experiences. How does one handle a skunk who is sharp and determined? How do you face a midnight meeting in a cemetery?

Gilson, Jamie
A3
Hobie Hanson, You're Weird
Lothrop, 1987

Hobie Hanson is looking forward to the summer. Instead of going away he is going to stay at home. He teams up with his school mate Molly Bosco and has a hilarious time.

Gilson, Jamie
A4
Double Dog Dare
Lothrop, 1988

Because he wants to be "someone" Hobie feels he must make a name for himself. Nick was at Computer Camp, Molly is talented and Lisa is popular. But what is Harvey? Could he outwit Molly?

Gipson, Fred
1
Old Yeller
Harper, 1956

Travis loved his yellow-colored dog and tried to tame and then train him as a hunting dog. Old Yeller made him proud.

Gipson, Fred
2
Savage Sam
Harper, 1962

Savage Sam is the son of Old Yeller. He helps Travis rescue Arliss from the Indians.

Gipson, Fred
3
Little Arliss
Harper, 1978

By looking for a runaway horse, Arliss hopes to prove his worthiness. Travis is grown and married. Arliss is 12 and has a troubling temper.

Glaser, Dianne
1
Amber Wellington, Daredevil
Walker, 1975

Amber is the only girl in a mysterious and dangerous club: The Daredevils. When Old Larnie dies his money is missing! Should the Daredevils be concerned?

Glaser, Dianne
2
Amber Wellington, Witch Watcher
Walker, 1976

At midnight, Amber stands outside an old house and the Jewel Sisters adventure begins. Are they witches?

Gondosch, Linda
1
Who Needs a Bratty Brother?
Dutton, 1985

Kelly thinks her brother Ben is more than a pest. She tries to get rid of him by giving him to a neighbor, sending him to camp, enrolling him in a private school. When he runs away she is upset.

Gondosch, Linda
2
Witches of Hopper Street
Dutton, 1986

Kelly, Jennifer and Adelaide form a witch club and try to cast spells and fly on brooms. But there is a threat from someone else. In the end they find that Rae Jean is not so bad after all.

Gondosch, Linda
3
Who's Afraid of Haggerty House?
Dutton, 1987

Kelly had a fight with her two best friends, Jennifer and Adelaide. She meets Mrs. Haggerty, a strange old woman and spends time in her old house. But she misses her friends and wants to make up.

Graber, Richard
1
Little Breathing Room
Harper, 1978

When Ray and his younger brother fight, Ray is always blamed. He spends the summer with his grandparents to see if that can ease the tension at home.

Graber, Richard
2
Pay Your Respects
Harper, 1979

Ray and his friend Floyd are seniors. Floyd is emotionally unstable; he seriously injures his foot. Ray's parent problem continues. His grandmother dies and Ray decides to leave town.

Graber, Richard
3
Black Cow Summer
Harper, 1980

Ray, now 16, falls in love with a girl whose older brothers won't let him near her. He still has parent problems at home.

Greene, Bette
1
Philip Hall Likes Me.
I Reckon Maybe
Dial, 1974

As the number two student in school, Beth gets through a year of funny incidents because she doesn't want to beat out her friend, Philip Hall.

Greene, Bette
2
Get on Out of Here, Philip Hall
Dial, 1981

Beth is now trying to outdo Philip Hall and learns a valuable lesson about leadership when Philip gets the award she was sure was hers.

Greene, Bette
A1
Summer of My German Soldier
Dial, 1973

The heartbreaking story of a friendship between a Jewish girl, Patty, and a young escaped German POW during World War II. She hides him but he is found and shot. She must pay the price.

Greene, Bette
A2
Morning Is a Long Time Coming
Dial, 1978

The continuing story of Patty as she grows up, leaves high school, goes to Germany to find the family of the German POW, and finally settles her own life with a romance in Paris.

Greene, Constance
1
Girl Called Al
Viking, 1969

A traveling father, a divorced mother and too much fat tells the story of Al and her best friend who live in the same apartment building.

Greene, Constance
2
I Know You, Al
Viking, 1975

Al and her best friend cope with, among other things, Al's weight, her mother and her boyfriend and her father's remarriage.

Greene, Constance
3
Your Old Pal, Al
Viking, 1979

Al and her best friend wait for letters from both Brian, a boy she knows, and Al's father's new wife but a house guest, Polly, confuses things.

Greene, Constance
4
Al(exandra) the Great
Viking, 1982

Al must give up a summer visit with her father to take care of her mother who is sick, and she gets a T-shirt with "Al(exandra) the Great" on it. She also meets a boy she likes.

Greene, Constance
5
Just Plain Al
Viking, 1986

Two teenage girls, Al and her friend, cope with life in a New York City apartment. Some days are good, some days are bad.

Greene, Constance
A1
Isabelle, the Itch
Viking, 1973

Isabelle's brother's paper route help her become more popular, which is what she is after.

Greene, Constance
A2
Isabelle Shows Her Stuff
Viking, 1984

Guy and Isabelle team up to make Guy a "better pest." They both learn a lesson from this experience.

Greene, Constance
A3
Isabelle and Little Orphan Frannie
Viking, 1988
Isabelle would like to be as popular as Mary Elizabeth but isn't. But she does help Frannie who can't read by trying to teach her.

Gripe, Marie
1
Hugo and Josephine
Delacorte, 1969
The hilarious adventures of two young children as they attend school. Josephine is unhappy because she is teased and Hugo, a happy boy defends her. They become close friends.

Gripe, Marie
2
Josephine
Delacorte, 1970
Josephine, being one of seven children, feels unwanted and runs away from home. She meets Granny Lyra, finds her threatening and hurries home to security.

Gripe, Marie
3
Hugo
Delacorte, 1970
Hugo lives in the woods with his father and sometimes goes to school with his friend, Josephine. Most of the time he tries to earn money with little success.

Gripe, Marie
A1
Night Daddy
Delacorte, 1968
A story told chapter by chapter of the friendship between Julia, a young girl, and Peter, her sitter. Peter is a writer and Julia has no father.

Gripe, Marie
A2
Julia's House
Delacorte, 1975
As Julia grows older she still has a relationship with Peter but each is jealous of the friends of the other. But they work together when it appears that Julia's house is to be torn down.

Guy, Rosa
1
Friends
Holt, 1973
Phyllisia recognizes the reason for the conflict between herself and her best friend, Edith. She is so different but she is loyal and helps Phyl stand up to her father.

Guy, Rosa
2
Ruby
Viking, 1976
The continuing story of the two Black teenagers, Phyllisia and Ruby. Phyl studies hard at school and Ruby makes friends with Daphne.

Guy, Rosa
3
Edith Jackson
Viking, 1978
Edith tries to keep her sisters together but they leave their foster home and reject her efforts. Edith must make her own life.

Guy, Rosa
A1
Disappearance
Delacorte, 1979
The disappearance of seven-year-old Perk in Brooklyn casts suspicion on a juvenile offender in Harlem: Imamu Jones.

Guy, Rosa
A2
New Guy Around the Block
Delacorte, 1983
Imamu suspects one of his friends of committing crimes. He also tries to cope with an alcoholic mother.

Hallard, Peter
1
Coral Reef Castaways
Criterion, 1958
Sixteen-year-old Con Murray is swept overboard and swims to a reef where Gentry has his oyster bed. He and Con attempt to make money from these. Someone else tries to claim and work the beds.

Hallard, Peter
2
Barrier Reef Bandit
Critorion, 1960
Real pearls are in a safe of a sunken ship. Con and Gentry search for and salvage the ship.

Hamilton, Virginia
1
Justice and Her Brothers
Greenwillow, 1979
Justice and Thomas and Levi struggle to understand their super-sensory powers. They find they can travel to the future. They are joined by a fourth child, Dorian, who is also extrasensory.

Hamilton, Virginia
2
Dustland
Greenwillow, 1980
Bound together by extraordinary mind power, three teens are hurtled into the future to Dustland where everything is dust. Slaker, a dustwalker, meets Justice and she reads his mind.

Hamilton, Virginia
3
Gathering
Greenwillow, 1981
These four teenagers with super-sensory powers, linked together, each with distinct powers and talents, return to Dustland and fight for the control of the future.

Hamilton, Virginia
A1
House of Dies Drear
Macmillan, 1968
A Black family, the Small's, bought an old house full of passageways and discover a treasure in an abandoned cave. It was an old underground railway station.

Hamilton, Virginia
A2
Mystery of Drear House
Greenwillow, 1987
Thomas Small and his family are cataloging the treasures they found on their land. But the question arises: To whom does this treasure belong?

Hamner, Earl
1
Spencer's Mountain
Dial, 1961
A legendary white deer lives on Spencer's Mountain, where the Spencer family has lived for generations. This is the story of Clay-Boy and his eight brothers and sisters.

Hamner, Earl
2
Homecoming
Random, 1970
Clay-boy, the eldest son, went to look for his father when he didn't return home on time. He met with a snowstorm, Blacks, bootleggers and the Sheriff. The father is losing all hope.

Harris, Christie
1
You Have to Draw
the Line Somewhere
Atheneum, 1964
A girl, Linsey, grows up in an unusual home, and becomes an artist.

Harris, Christie
2
Confessions of a Toe-Hanger
Atheneum, 1967
Feeny, Linsey's sister, does not have the talent and poise that Linsey has. But needs to make her own life.

Harris, Geraldine
1
Prince of Godborn
Greenwillow, 1983
Kerish sets out to find the sorcerer behind the Seven Gates.

Harris, Geraldine
2
Children of the Wind
Greenwillow, 1983
Kerish travels through deadly Lan-Pin-Fria to get the keys needed for his search.

Harris, Geraldine
3
Dead Kingdom
Greenwillow, 1983

Kerish and his friends are still looking for the keys held by the sorcerer.

Harris, Geraldine
4
Seventh Gate
Greenwillow, 1984
Kerish and his friend have nearly found the keys when they are captured by Fanfmere.

Harris, Rosemary
1
Moon in the Cloud
Macmillan, 1968
Comical version of how Noah's son Ham and dedicated friend were able to assemble the animals on the ark, especially two Temple cats.

Harris, Rosemary
2
Shadow on the Sun
Macmillan, 1970
What happens when Ruben returned to Kemi with his animals after the flood subsided.

Harris, Rosemary
3
Bright and Morning Star
Macmillan, 1972
Some years later Ruben becomes Merenkere's musician.

Harris, Rosemary
A1
Quest for Orion
Faber & Faber, 1978
A group of teenagers in 1999 fight against being subjugated by political decisions. They are helped by some magical relics of Charlemagne and, of course, from the constellation Orion.

Harris, Rosemary
A2
Tower of the Stars
Faber & Faber, 1980
This continues the story of the political intrigue of the future: some practical events and some magical and fantastic ones.

Haugaard, Erik
1

Hakon of Rogen's Saga
Houghton, 1963
Hakon is the heir of Rogen Island but his uncle takes him captive on the death of his father. He waits until he can escape and return home.

Haugaard, Erik
2
Slave's Tale
Houghton, 1965
Hakon sails for Brittany but encounters storms. He finds a stowaway girl, Helga, and tries to get Rark, a former slave back to his homeland. It's a dangerous trip with many harrowing adventures.

Haugaard, Erik
A1
Messenger for Parliament
Houghton, 1976
A story of the English Civil War between Charles I, Cromwell and the Puritans. Oliver and his father face the hardships of war and Oliver hides in a demolished church.

Haugaard, Erik
A2
Cromwell's Boy
Houghton, 1978
Oliver becomes Cromwell's messenger because he can ride fast and can be trusted to be loyal. He survives as a spy by using his intelligence and horsemanship.

Hearn, Betsy
1
South Star
Atheneum, 1977
Megan is a giant who escapes death when her parents are killed. She meets Randall and the Bear and escapes from the Screamer.

Hearn, Betsy
2
Home
Atheneum, 1979
Megan searches for the lost king of the giants, Brendan. Randall helps her find Brendan and free him from his captors.

Heide, Florence
1
Mystery of the Silver Tag
Whitman, 1972
When a valuable cat is obviously missing, the Spotlight Club sets out to rescue it.

Heide, Florence
2
Mystery of the Missing Suitcase
Whitman, 1972
When they pick up the wrong suitcase, the Spotlight Club members are involved in a bank robbery.

Heide, Florence
3
Hidden Box Mystery
Whitman, 1973
Jay, Cindy and Dexter are looking for a petty thief. But a valuable chess piece is missing from the museum. The Spotlight Club must get help.

Heide, Florence
4
Mystery of the Macadoo Zoo
Whitman, 1973
Spotlight Club members track down a pickpocket who is running loose in the zoo.

Heide, Florence
5
Mystery of the Melting Snowman
Whitman, 1974
Spotlight detectives are involved with a mysterious man and an iron dog.

Heide, Florence
6
Mystery of the Whispering Voice
Whitman, 1974
The Spotlight Club sees a newcomer as suspicious because he whispers.

Heide, Florence
7
Deadline for McGurk
Whitman, 1974
There is a rash of doll-nappings taking place and the Spotlight Club, Willie, Joey and Wanda must solve the crime.

Heide, Florence
8
Mystery of the Bewitched Bookmobile
Whitman, 1975
A Spotlight Club mystery about books and libraries.

Heide, Florence
9
Mystery of the Lonely Lantern
Whitman, 1976
There is a masked stranger in an empty house. He is the legal heir who is being cheated out of his inheritance. The Spotlight Club helps find the relatives who are responsible.

Heide, Florence
10
Mystery at Keyhold Carnival
Whitman, 1977
The Spotlight Club members help out at the carnival and find a counterfeiter.

Heide, Florence
11
Mystery at Southport Cinema
Whitman, 1978
Thorne lost a bag of money belonging to someone else. The thief ran into a cinema and did not come out. The Spotlight crew look for clues in the form of a disguise.

Heide, Florence
12
Mystery of the Forgotten Island
Whitman, 1979
Rowing on the lake the Spotlight detectives find an island where an old man is held captive.

Heide, Florence
13
Mystery of the Mummy's Mask
Whitman, 1979
The Spotlight Club gets involved with a dealer in old masks. It all started with of an ancient mask.

Heide, Florence
14
Mystery of the Midnight Message
Whitman, 1982
Cindy and Jay are stranded in a hotel

during a blizzard. They learn about a robbery which is to take place nearby.

Heide, Florence
15
Mystery of the Vanishing Visitor
Whitman, 1982

A burglar robs a neighbor's house looking for a painting of a cat that has money hidden in it. Another case for the Spotlight Club.

Heide, Florence
16
Mystery of the Danger Road
Whitman, 1983

Cindy goes to pick up clowns for a charity fair. She picks up the wrong ones. She also rescues an injured dog. The thieves steal the clowns back and also take Cindy and the dog.

Heide, Florence
A1
Brillstone Break-in
Whitman, 1977

Two teenagers become involved with money delivered as a bribe to Eric, the officer at the housing development. Liza is the daughter of a newspaperman and an investigator.

Heide, Florence
A2
Burning Stone at Brillstone
Whitman, 1978

Liza and her journalistic friend, Logan, find that life at the Brillstone apartments is a series of suspicious events. Liza's reporter father is a source of information of these events.

Heide, Florence
A3
Fear at Brillstone
Whitman, 1978

Logan is hired by a theft-prone company where he learns about a robbery. He and Liza take pictures that are clues to the robbery and then someone is after the film.

Heide, Florence
A4
Face at the Brillstone Window

Whitman, 1979

Liza's father is a crime reporter who specializes in young first offenders. Liza wants to clear Robin of a robbery she feels he didn't do. Through the diary of a ten-year-old, she does.

Heide, Florence
A5
Black Magic at Brillstone
Whitman, 1981

A fast-paced, suspenseful mystery with Logan and Liza at the Brillstone apartments.

Heide, Florence
A6
Time Bomb at Brillstone
Whitman, 1982

Liza finds that not all crimes can be prevented or solved all the time. A slight change from most amateur detective stories.

Heide, Florence
A7
Body in the Brillstone Garage
Whitman, 1988

Liza discovers a body but when she returns with a friend the body is gone. Who is the murderer? Is it the man with the jacket? She recognizes the shirt of Mr. Greening but he's alive.

Heide, Florence
B1
Time's Up
Holiday, 1982

Noah's mother and father are too busy for him. He dreams of owning a bike. He meets his new neighbor, Bib, and gains a friend (and a bike).

Heide, Florence
B2
Time Flies
Holiday, 1984

Noah just knows the new baby is going to be troublesome, especially as he sees Bib and her family. But he finally ends up being proud of his sister.

Heide, Florence
C1
Shrinking of Treehorn

Holiday, 1971

Treehorn needs to decide whether he wants to be green or small. The only way to stop himself from shrinking is to play a magical game that turns him green.

Heide, Florence
C2
Treehorn's Treasure
Holiday, 1981

One day a tree has dollar bills for leaves. Treehorn uses it to buy comic books and candy. No one believes him when he tells about the tree. But it begins to go back to normal leaves.

Heide, Florence
C3
Treehorn's Wish
Holiday, 1984

Treehorn finds a genie in a bottle and is granted wishes. He wishes for a birthday cake that his parents failed to provide.

Henry, Marguerite
1
Misty of Chincoteague
Rand McNally, 1947

Outstanding classic story about an unusual horse bought at an auction.

Henry, Marguerite
2
Sea Star
Rand McNally, 1949

Misty was sold to be shared with children everywhere. Paul and Maureen find a stray colt on the beach and save its life.

Henry, Marguerite
3
Stormy, Misty's Foal
Rand McNally, 1963

Misty's foal is born in the aftermath of a great storm that ravaged the Chincoteague Island. Thus the name Stormy.

Hentoff, Nat
1
This School Is Driving Me Crazy
Delacorte, 1976

Sam doesn't want to go to school where his father is headmaster; but he causes more trouble than he intended.

Hentoff, Nat
2
Does This School Have Capital Punishment?
Delacorte, 1981

Sam really has his troubles at school, some humorous, some adventurous, but all still trouble. His project about a jazz musician and a bully fellow student are the cause of some of it.

Hermes, Patricia
1
Kevin Corbett Eats Flies
Harcourt, 1986

Kevin and Bailey want to prevent Kevin's father (and Kevin) from moving away again.

Hermes, Patricia
2
Heads, I Win
Harcourt, 1988

Bailey, living in a foster home, hopes running for class president will help her situation.

Hermes, Patricia
A1
What If They Knew?
Harcourt, 1980

Jeremy is staying with grandparents while her parents are away. She has epilepsy. Her new friends find out and accept it.

Hermes, Patricia
A2
Place for Jeremy
Harcourt, 1987

Jeremy is staying with her grandparents longer than expected. She must now start at a new school. She finds out that her absent parents have adopted a baby sister.

Heuman, William
1
Horace Higby and the Scientific Pitch
Dodd, 1968

An unusual boy, Horace Higby, in a story about baseball. It is a science fantasy with some facts and a lot of imagination.

Heuman, William
2
Horace Higby
and the Field Goal Formula
Dodd, 1969
The same unusual Horace Higby but this time science and fantasy are involved in football.

Heuman, William
3
Horace Higby
and the Gentle Fullback
Dodd, 1970
Horace Higby is still involved in sports with his unusual scientific approach.

Heuman, William
4
Horace Higby, Coxswain of the Crew
Dodd, 1971
This time the sport is rowing. After trying baseball and football Horace is ready for something different.

Hickman, Janet
1
Stones
Macmillan, 1976
While his father is fighting in World War II, Garrett McKay harasses an old German man.

Hickman, Janet
2
Thunder-Pup
Macmillan, 1981
Linnie McKay hopes to get a puppy for her birthday, but she messes up at school; Darle, the snob, appears; and her present is her parents' new house. But she does get her puppy, eventually.

Hicks, Clifford
1
Marvelous Inventions of Alvin Fernald
Holt, 1960
Alvin invents the Sure Shot Paper Slinger and the fun and trouble begins in the Old Huntley (haunted?) Place. There are strange footprints in the dust.

Hicks, Clifford
2
Alvin's Secret Code
Houghton, 1963
Alvin is Secret Agent 12½. He and his friend Shoie break a secret code to save an orphanage. His sister, the Pest, helps. They find a treasure buried during the Civil War.

Hicks, Clifford
3
Alvin Fernald, Foreign Trader
Holt, 1966
Alvin wins a candy cooking contest: A trip to Europe. He has some very funny adventures with Shole and the Pest who, of course, goes too.

Hicks, Clifford
4
Alvin Fernald, Mayor for a Day
Holt, 1970
Alvin wins the right to be the mayor for a day but finds out that the mayor is a criminal. A funny spoof on kids and the SYSTEM.

Hicks, Clifford
5
Alvin Fernald, Superweasel
Holt, 1974
Alvin's pollution project is geared to expose the biggest polluter in town—the owner of the chemical plant.

Hicks, Clifford
6
Alvin's Swap Shop
Holt, 1976
Alvin starts a Swap Shop with one black ant traded for some dead spiders and the shop becomes a hideout for a fugitive, Pim. They all team up to capture a criminal.

Hicks, Clifford
7
Alvin Fernald, T.V. Anchorman
Holt, 1980
Alvin solves an 11-year-old mystery while he earns a regular spot on the television news. He proves a cameraman's innocence and reunites him with his son, all on television.

Hicks, Clifford
8
Wacky World of Alvin Fernald
Holt, 1981
This "brainy" boy now turns a bicycle into an airplane. He also pulls an April Fool's joke on his home town.

Hicks, Clifford
9
*Alvin Fernald, Master
of a Thousand Disguises*
Holt, 1986
Is the Huntley Place really haunted? Alvin thinks not. However, how is he going to prove or disprove it?

Hicks, Clifford
A1
Peter Potts
Dutton, 1971
Everything he does is wrong. Why won't his schemes work? Peter and Joey want to surprise Joey's mother but shock her instead. The April Fool's Day trick with the spider backfires.

Hicks, Clifford
A2
Pops and Peter Potts
Holt, 1984
Peter and his grandfather, Pops, have more schemes and hobbies that are hilarious and exciting, such as lion taming (backwards) and hypnotizing chickens.

Highwater, Jamake
1
Legend Days
Harper, 1984
Grandfather Fox passes on to 11-year-old Amana the intrinsic qualities of a hunter's instinct and a warrior's prowess.

Highwater, Jamake
2
Ceremony of Innocence
Harper, 1985
After being disillusioned by the death of her husband, Amana finds friendship and love. She instills the pride of Indian heritage in her daughter.

Highwater, Jamake
3
I Wear the Morning Star
Harper, 1986
Sitko, an Indian, learns to paint and keep his Indian heritage as he lives among Whites.

Hildick, E. W.
1
Nose Knows
Whitman, 1973
A fast, funny, easy reading mystery with Jack McGurk. This is the first of many others. Willie is the Nose.

Hildick, E. W.
2
Case of the Nervous Newsboy
Macmillan, 1976
The police help McGurk and his fellow detectives, Joey, Wanda and Willie, find a runaway newsboy.

Hildick, E. W.
3
Great Rabbit Rip-off
Macmillan, 1977
One of four detectives, Wanda, is accused of defacing and then stealing all the ornamental clay rabbits in the neighborhood. Willie, the Nose, is a big help in this adventure.

Hildick, E. W.
4
Case of the Invisible Dog
Macmillan, 1977
McGurk matches wits with a very young scientific genius before he is able to solve the mystery of the invisible dog.

Hildick, E. W.
5
Case of the Condemned Cat
Macmillan, 1978
The suspect in this mystery is Whiskers, the pet cat; the crime is murder; the victim, a white dove; and the penalty, to the local pound if guilty.

Hildick, E. W.
6
Case of the Secret Scribbler
Macmillan, 1978
McGurk finds a suspicious slip of

paper in a library book. It turns out to be a mysterious map and a crime yet to be committed.

Hildick, E. W.
7
Case of the Phantom Frog
Macmillan, 1979

McGurk stumbles on a frightening puzzle who—or what—is making snarling, unearthly sounds. Who is under the mask?

Hildick, E. W.
8
Case of the Treetop Treasure
Macmillan, 1980

In this case one of McGurk's own "men" is the suspect in a burglary. While rescuing a killer they find "treasure." But a valuable stolen bowl does show up among the treasures."

Hildick, E. W.
9
Case of the Snowbound Spy
Macmillan, 1980

The McGurk organization is now involved in espionage at a very high level. They carry messages and packages unwittingly.

Hildick, E. W.
10
Case of the Bashful Bank Robber
Macmillan, 1981

Armed robbers are coming to town, and McGurk and his organization is on red alert. They learn about it from a photo taken at the bank earlier.

Hildick, E. W.
11
Case of the Four Flying Fingers
Macmillan, 1981

A burglar, and a group of children who unwittingly help him, runs afoul of McGurk's organization.

Hildick, E. W.
12
Case of the Felon's Fiddle
Macmillan, 1982

A note in a violin and uncut diamonds are McGurk's clues in this mystery.

Hildick, E. W.
13
McGurk Gets Good and Mad
Macmillan, 1982

Someone sabotages McGurk's First Annual Open House. He is really "good and mad" when his special handcuffs are stolen.

Hildick, E. W.
14
Case of the Slingshot Sniper
Macmillan, 1983

The McGurk Detective Organization competes against a clairvoyant rival while attempting to solve a case of vandalism.

Hildick, E. W.
15
Case of the Vanishing Ventriloquist
Macmillan, 1985

The McGurk organization must act to prevent a crime, but they don't know what the crime will be. Another member joins the group and helps solve this one. Mari joins the organization.

Hildick, E. W.
16
Case of the Muttering Mummy
Macmillan, 1986

The cat Joey bought at a museum gets the attention of an expert on Egyptian artifacts and therefore the attention of the McGurk organization.

Hildick, E. W.
17
Case of the Wandering Weathervanes
Macmillan, 1988

An enemy agent is followed by McGurk to find out who is stealing the weathervanes and why.

Hildick, E. W.
A1
Ghost Squad Breaks Through
Dutton, 1984

Ghosts band together to both solve and prevent crimes when one of them, Danny, finds he can communicate with two living beings, Wacko and Buzz, through a computer.

Hildick, E. W.
A2
Ghost Squad Flies Concorde
Dutton, 1985
The four ghosts that make up the Ghost Squad fly to England to investigate a swindle.

Hildick, E. W.
A3
Ghost Squad
and the Halloween Conspiracy
Dutton, 1985
The Ghost Squad must prevent unscrupulous people, like Vinnie, from putting needles into chocolates on Halloween. Malevs, the "bad" ghosts enter the picture.

Hildick, E. W.
A4
Ghost Squad
and the Ghoul of Grunberg
Dutton, 1986
The ghost Squad helps investigate the happenings at a rich summer camp. They find that the owner is a missing Nazi war leader.

Hildick, E. W.
A5
Ghost Squad
and the Prowling Hermits
Dutton, 1987
The four ghosts prevent evil Dr. Purcell's plan to have a ghost take over living bodies, from going into effect.

Hildick, E. W.
A6
Ghost Squad
and the Menace of the Malevs
Dutton, 1988
The Ghost Squad can't believe that "nice" Clem Jackson is Joe's murderer. Again they must face Grunberg, leader of the evil ghosts, the Malevs.

Hill, Douglas
1
Exiles of Colsac
Atheneum, 1984
Twelve rebel youngsters crash-land on an alien planet; six of them survive, one is a killer. Cord is their leader.

Hill, Douglas
2
Caves of Klydor
Atheneum, 1985
Cord and the other young rebels are exiled to the planet Klydor.

Hill, Douglas
3
Colsac Rebellion
Atheneum, 1985
The teenagers exiled to the planet Klydor return to Earth and lead a rebellion.

Hill, Douglas
A1
Huntsman
Atheneum, 1982
Finn Ferral begins his adventure with the evil Slavers who want to conquer the Earth.

Hill, Douglas
A2
Warriors of the Wasteland
Atheneum, 1983
Finn Ferral searches for Jena, who was captured by Slavers. He is pursued by Claw.

Hill, Douglas
A3
Alien Citadel
Atheneum, 1984
Finn, captured by the cruel Slavers, learns the truth at last about these alien rulers of Earth, and the secret of the Citadel.

Hill, Douglas
B1
Galactic Warlord
Atheneum, 1980
Keill must find the "evil intelligence" that everyone believes is responsible for the destruction of Moros and its people. He must avenge this wrong.

Hill, Douglas
B2
Day of the Starwind
Atheneum, 1981
Moros and his alien companion set a course for the uninhabited planet of

Rilyn, to investigate the sinister activities of the Warlord and his agent, the Deathwing.

Hill, Douglas
B3
Deathwing over Veynaa
Atheneum, 1981
Deathwing is the agent of the Warlord who rules Rilyn and is the doer of evil.

Hill, Douglas
B4
Planet of the Warlord
Atheneum, 1982
Keill, the Last Legionary, and his alien friend, Gir, are left alive on Moros, the destroyed planet. They are in deep trouble as they face the "evil genius" that is responsible.

Hill, Douglas
B5
Young Legionary
Atheneum, 1983
Keill survives a test and is selected for training to fight savage life on an alien planet.

Hill, Douglas
C1
Blade of the Poisoners
McElderry, 1987
Jarrel is tainted by an evil sword which must be destroyed or he will die.

Hill, Douglas
C2
Master of the Fiends
McElderry, 1988
Jarrel sets out to rescue the wizard, Cryttaun, from the palace of demons.

Hinton, S. E.
1
Outsiders
Viking, 1967
The Greasers are a bunch of tough boys who fight with a rival gang, the Socs. Johnny and Ponyboy hide out after one of the Socs is killed. They save a child from death but Ponyboy dies.

Hinton, S. E.
2

That Was Then, This Is Now
Viking, 1971
Byron, a Greaser, lives with Mark and his family. He finds out that Mark is on drugs and he is faced with turning him in. He cares about his future but Mark is still doing things for "kicks."

Hodges, C. W.
1
Namesake
Coward, 1964
This is the story of Alfred the Great, King of England and his fight against the invaders of England. His leniency with the Danish King, Guthorm, is questioned when Guthorm seeks revenge.

Hodges, C. W.
2
Marsh King
Coward, 1967
King Alfred barely escapes from Somerset Marshes as an ambush is attempted. A great deal is learned about life in England at that time. A true historical novel.

Hodges, Margaret
1
Hatching of Joshua Cobb
Farrar, 1967
Josh is at summer camp with a counselor who is a bully. There is a great deal of humor in Josh's sleep-away camp, after the bully is dismissed and replaced.

Hodges, Margaret
2
Making of Joshua Cobb
Farrar, 1971
Josh is an eighth grader with lots of friends. He has some great adventures in sports and other school activities. This boarding school could help him but can he make it?

Hodges, Margaret
3
Freewheeling of Joshua Cobb
Farrar, 1974
One could predict Josh's bicycle camping trip would not be untroubled. Five friends on a ten-day camping trip is

bound to be unpredictable. But even Cassandra proves her mettle.

Holmes, Barbara
1
Charlotte Cheetham:
Master of Disaster
Harper, 1985
Charlotte tells lies. To win friendship with Tina she tells a whopper: that her friend owns a sticker factory and she will take them there for a visit. Her friend Anna helps her out of it.

Holmes, Barbara
2
Charlotte the Starlet
Harper, 1988
Charlotte is going to write. Everyone likes what she writes. She is a star! But, is it real? Her best friend Annie says, No, she is being used because of what she writes. She throws the book away.

Holmvik, Oyvind
1
Dive to Danger
Harcourt, 1964
A group of boys including very spoiled Lars are taught to be skin divers; and spies!

Holmvik, Oyvind
2
Crack of Doom
Harcourt, 1966
An exciting story of the skin diver's struggle with the sea. As frogmen they repair a ruptured dam. They also rescue people in the path of the flood.

Honeycutt, Natalie
1
All New Jonah Twist
Bradbury, 1986
Jonah has trouble with being on time, trouble with trying to live up to his older brother, Todd and trouble with Granville, a fellow student who is a bully. But Jonah is going to change.

Honeycutt, Natalie
2
Best Laid Plans of Jonah Twist
Bradbury, 1988

Jonah and Granville become friends! Jonah wants a pet kitten and wants to find his brother's missing hamster. And he wants to keep Juliet out of his science project plans. He won't be stopped.

Honig, Donald
1
Jed McLane and Storm Cloud
McGraw-Hill, 1968
An exciting Western about Jed, a 14-year-old, and his horse. He lives on an Army base in 1880. He saved an innocent Indian boy from being hanged.

Honig, Donald
2
Jed McLane and the Stranger
McGraw-Hill, 1969
Jed's father was a good and admired solider but a stranger came looking for him with revenge as a motive.

Honness, Elizabeth
1
Mystery of the Auction Trunk
Lippincott, 1956
Nancy, Barby and Doug bid on an old trunk and become involved in an art mystery. It not only involves the former home of the artist but some very old paintings and unscrupulous art dealers.

Honness, Elizabeth
2
Mystery of the Wooden Indian
Lippincott, 1958
Nancy, Barby and Doug spend the Christmas holidays at the vacation home where they usually spend their summers. They discover a cigar store Indian in an old building and the mystery begins.

Hoover, H. M.
1
Children of Morrow
Four Winds, 1973
A story of two children born to parents from two different cultures and have powers of telepathy.

Hoover, H. M.
2

Treasures of Morrow
Four Winds, 1976
  These telepathic youngsters spend some time with the more advanced culture of one of their parents.

Hopkins, Lee
1
Mama
Knopf, 1977
  Mama takes things from where she works: clothes, meat, etc., to make ends meet. Her son, Chris, carries them home knowing it's wrong but can't do anything. Mama starts to work at a laundry.

Hopkins, Lee
2
Mama and Her Boys
Harper, 1981
  Mr. Jacobs of the laundry wants to marry Mama but she refuses. The school custodian, Mike, is interviewed by her son for the school newspaper and a friendship begins with Mama and Mike.

Horseman, Elaine
1
Hubble's Bubble
Norton, 1964
  Sarah and Alaric have an old book of magic spells. They can turn themselves and others into cats, mice and toads. They can fly over the city. Charlotte, Jonathan and Peter join in the fun.

Horseman, Elaine
2
Hubble's Treasure Hunt
Norton, 1965
  Sarah and Alaric go on a treasure hunt with Charlotte, Peter and Jonathan when Sarah found a note in an old inherited doll. Their magic spell book takes them back in time to the Civil War.

Houston, James
1
Frozen Fire
Atheneum, 1977
  Matthew's father is lost in an Arctic storm. Matthew and Kayak, his friend,

go to look for him. The trip is dangerous and they run out of gas for their snowmobile before they reach home.

Houston, James
2
Black Diamonds
Atheneum, 1982
  While returning home they find gold nuggets. When Matthew's father does reach home they all set out to find the mother lode of these nuggets. Is it "black diamonds" as oil is known up there?

Houston, James
A1
White Archer
Harcourt, 1967
  Kungo lost his parents in a massacre. He wants revenge. But when the time comes to inflict it, he has doubts.

Houston, James
A2
Falcon Bow
McElderry, 1986
  Kungo finds the Inuit people starving because of the loss of the caribou. Something must be done about the ecological chain.

Howe, James
1
Bunnicula
Atheneum, 1979
  Bunnicula is a vampire bunny. He was found in a shoe box at the movies. Harold, the dog and Chester, the cat know he's no ordinary rabbit.

Howe, James
2
Howliday Inn
Atheneum, 1982
  Harold and Chester, a dog and a cat, are in the crime detection business.

Howe, James
3
Celery Stalks at Midnight
Atheneum, 1983
  Chester the cat is now more than ever convinced that Bunnicula is a vampire when more white vegetables show up.

Howe, James
4
Nighty-Nightmare
Atheneum 1987

Harold and Chester are on a camping trip with the Monroe's. They sniff that there's going to be trouble. They're right. Bud, Spud and their dog are bad news.

Howe, James
A1
What Eric Knew
Atheneum, 1986

Eric sends cryptic notes to his friends who investigate a mysterious death. A Sebastian Barth mystery.

Howe, James
A2
Stage Fright
Atheneum, 1986

Sebastian Barth is involved in a theatre mystery. There are warnings and some strange accidents as a famous actress comes to visit his home town. "House of Cards" seems jinxed.

Howe, James
A3
Eat Your Poison, Dear
Atheneum, 1986

Students become ill after eating in the school cafeteria. The school officials say it is the flu but Sebastian and David say it is not and solve the mystery of Milo and Miss Swille.

Huddy, Delia
1
Time Piper
Greenwillow, 1979

Luke leaves London to work with Tom Humbolt, the inventor of a revolutionary time machine. He finds the children of the Pied Piper of Hamlin and restores their souls.

Huddy, Delia
2
Humboldt Effect
Greenwillow, 1982

A submarine trip in the Mediterranean has cataclysmic results when a team member is lost at sea and a man from the fourth century is taken aboard.

Hughes, Dean
1
Nutty for President
Atheneum 1981

William, the new boy in school, is going to make Nutty, a fifth grader, president of the Student Council even though that position has always been held by sixth graders.

Hughes, Dean
2
Nutty and the Case
of the Mastermind Thief
Atheneum, 1985

Nutty and his friend William get together to solve a crime. It appears that William has talents as yet unheard of but there are always strings attached to his activities.

Hughes, Dean
3
Nutty and the Case
of the Ski Slope Spy
Atheneum, 1985

Nutty as Student Council president manages a ski trip for the school holiday. He finds stolen computer plans in his hotel room and hides them again. He waits for a message from "Russian Roulette."

Hughes, Dean
4
Nutty Can't Miss
Atheneum, 1987

Nutty plays basketball at the recreation center. He plays poorly until William helps him by programming him to be an excellent player. Nutty begins to wonder if he really wants this.

Hughes, Dean
5
Nutty Knows All
Atheneum, 1988

Nutty wants the best science project but he only has two days left to complete it. William helps by changing Nutty's brain through light waves and photons. But it ends with Nutty well.

Hughes, Monica
1

Keeper of the Isis Light
Atheneum, 1981

Olwen lives on Isis with a robot, Guardian, who has raised her. When people from Earth come, she is upset but then falls tragically in love with Mark.

Hughes, Monica
2
Guardian of Isis
Atheneum, 1982

In 2136, Isis settlers lose all technical knowledge and revert to a more primitive life style. Mark is president of the Earth people. Jody tries to make simple machines, but is repulsed.

Hughes, Monica
3
Isis Peddler
Atheneum, 1983

Moira's rocket ship breaks down on a strange planet Isis, and the beings living there are threatened by her father. She and Guardian and a young man team up to stop him.

Hughes, Monica
A1
Devil on My Back
Atheneum, 1984

Only the Lords have access to the computer as the Earth begins to run out of fuel. Tomi, a Lord's son, gets Outside with the Slaves and works to overthrow Arcone.

Hughes, Monica
A2
Dream Catchers
Atheneum, 1987

Ruth, with ESP is an Outsider living in Ark Three, a domed city. Ark Three has used technology to enslave people. Ruth hears about trouble in another civilization and goes to help.

Hunter, Kristin
1
Soul Brother and Sister Lou
Scribner, 1968

Lou and members of the Hawks gang make music together in their clubhouse. She distrusts Whites and one of the gang members is killed even though the gang is warned by Lou.

Hunter, Kristin
2
Lou in the Limelight
Scribner, 1981

Lou and the Soul Brothers leave home hoping for quick success in show business. They cut a record that becomes a hit. But they find that life in a casino is full of stress and disloyalty.

Hunter, Mollie
1
Sound of Chariots
Harper, 1972

The story of a girl, Bridie, who loses her father when she is nine. She leads a sad, revengeful life. Then poverty adds to the trials of her life but she still wants to become a writer.

Hunter, Mollie
2
Hold on To Love
Harper, 1984

Bridie struggles to become a writer; she meets Peter, a classmate, and learns about love in terms of her independence and Peter's possessiveness.

Hurwitz, Joanna
1
Much Ado about Aldo
Morrow, 1978

Aldo's love of animals brings chaos to his life. He begins by raising crickets and chameleons only to find that chameleons eat crickets. He is devastated and refuses to eat any meat.

Hurwitz, Johanna
2
Aldo Applesauce
Morrow, 1979

Aldo moves from the city to a town, and is afraid. He has many mishaps. He has trouble making new friends.

Hurwitz, Johanna
3
Aldo Ice Cream
Morrow, 1981

Aldo loves ice cream. He tries to raise

money by selling homemade ice cream, but with little luck. He does volunteer work for senior citizens.

Hurwitz, Johanna
4
Tough-Luck Karen
Morrow, 1982

Karen is Aldo's sister. She believes that her luck is always bad. She doesn't like school and while doing a science project Karen finds her luck can sometimes be good or at least not bad.

Jansson, Tove
1
Finn Family Moomintroll
Walck, 1965

Same book as *The Happy Moomins.*

Jansson, Tove
1a
The Happy Moomins
Walck, 1952

This is the same book as *Finn Family Moomintroll.* It is the introductory book where we meet all the Moomins and Moominvalley.

Jansson, Tove
2
Moominsummer Madness
Walck, 1961

A volcano explodes and a tidal wave engulfs Moominvalley. The Moomin family escapes of a floating house.

Jansson, Tove
3
Moominland Midwinter
Walck, 1962

Moomins sleep during the winter. This year Moomintroll is fully awake so he wanders around. He meets many strange characters and learns about the winter habits of others.

Jansson, Tove
4
Tales from Moominvalley
Walck, 1964

The Moomin family is Moominpappa, Moominmamma, Moomintroll and Little My. They experience Christmas, a holiday unknown to them.

Jansson, Tove
5
Exploits of Moominpappa
Walck, 1966

Moominpappa relates the many adventures of his life. He starts with the time he ran away from the Home for Moomin Foundlings.

Jansson, Tove
6
Comet in Moominland
Walck, 1967

Moomintroll and Sniff go to investigate a comet that appears to be approaching and will collide with the Earth.

Jansson, Tove
7
Moominpappa at Sea
Walck, 1967

Pappa decides to move his family to an unusual island where vegetables seem to have strange ways of behaving.

Jansson, Tove
8
The Moomins in November
Walck, 1971

Six friends get together for winter in Moominvalley and visit with each other while they await the much loved Moomintroll family.

Johnston, Norma
1
Keeping Days
Atheneum, 1973

Tish and her mother fight constantly over Tish's friends, both girl and boy. Tish has to cope with loyalty and ethics. As one child among a large family she looks forward to high school.

Johnston, Norma
2
Glory in the Flower
Atheneum, 1974

As Tish grows older she learns to cope with her family. She has the lead in Romeo and Juliet and understands friendship. Her mother has another baby and Tish faces the next year.

Johnston, Norma
3
Sanctuary Tree
Atheneum, 1977
Tish has a great many situations to cope with at 15. Her friend, Ken, moves away, her father is ill, her grandfather dies and her sister has a baby.

Johnston, Norma
4
Mustard Seed of Magic
Atheneum, 1977
Tish still wants to be a writer. Her parents fight, her boyfriend has moved away and Tish must defend herself and her friends.

Johnston, Norma
5
Nice Girl Like You
Atheneum, 1980
Sara, Tish's niece, defends Paul against the hypocrisies of West Farm. Through Sara we learn about Tish's last 15 years.

Johnston, Norma
6
Myself and I
Atheneum, 1981
Paul moves to California because he needs to try to find out who his parents are. He returns and courts Sara. The history of all families, Tish's, Sara's and Paul's is revealed.

Johnston, Norma
A1
Carlisle's Hope
Bantam, 1986
Jess is sad when her Aunt Faith is killed in an accident and Cousin Virginia comes to live with them.

Johnston, Norma
A2
To Jess, with Love and Memories
Bantam, 1986
Jess' younger sister is flunking school and finds out she is adopted.

Johnston, Norma
A3
Carlisle's All
Bantam, 1986
Jess' father and mother go to the Middle East and she learns that the Embassy has been attacked by terrorists. Is her father alive? Everyone waits anxiously to find out.

Johnston, Norma
B1
Of Time and Seasons
Atheneum, 1975
Bridget's family is very talented. Father and a younger sibling paint, Mother and another sibling write, her twin brother plays piano and her other brother is a born leader. What about her?

Johnston, Norma
B2
Striving After Wind
Atheneum, 1976
Bridget tries very hard to establish herself as a person among her talented family. She learns to handle very difficult people, especially an older actor friend and a young male friend.

Johnston, Norma
C1
Swallows Song
Atheneum, 1978
Allison Standish is living as girls did in the 1920s. She is not proud of her reputation among her family and friends and wonders what to do about it.

Johnston, Norma
C2
If You Love Me, Let Me Go
Atheneum, 1978
Allison is 16 and wants to change her image but her family and friends don't see the change. Her new friend Lisa, sees her as she wants to be seen. She got more changes than expected.

Jones, Adrienne
1
Whistle Down a Dark Lane
Harper, 1982
A novel of female rights, prejudices and love. A mother and two daughters learn to cope when the husband/father

leaves them and they adjust emotionally, economically and socially.

Jones, Adrienne
?
Matter of Spunk
Harper, 1983

The continuing story of the determination, the courage and the humor of these females who survive life's adventures. The setting is Hollywood with its many unconventional characters.

Jones, Diana
1
Cart and Cwidder
Atheneum, 1977

Clennen the Singer and his family travel Dalemark giving shows and telling news. He is an Informer and is killed. Two of his children escape to the North but not before enduring troubles.

Jones, Diana
2
Drowned Amnet
Atheneum, 1977

Mitt plots the revenge of his father's "death." He hides away on a sailboat which is threatened and then saved by sea gods. The shipwrecked sailor he picks up is his father, a betrayer.

Jones, Diana
3
Spellcoats
Atheneum, 1979

This story also takes place in Dalemark. It is about an earlier time and explains the relationships of people, power and the gods during a time of great suspiciousness.

Kastner, Erich
1
Emil and the Detectives
Doubleday, 1930

Emil's friend, Gustav, and his friends, chase and catch the man who has robbed Emil in the train station.

Kastner, Erich
2
Emil and the Three Twins
Watts, 1961

Emil is called up to solve a mystery. A member of the Three Twins acrobatic team is unaccountably deserted by his father.

Kastner, Erich
A1
Little Man
Knopf, 1966

Maxie is only two inches tall and wants to be a circus performer. He does so, is kidnapped and outwits his captors and returns to the circus where he is warmly welcomed.

Kastner, Erich
A2
Little Man and the Big Thief
Knopf, 1969

Maxie, a two-inch tall man, becomes a circus entertainer and now is making a movie about himself. Another tiny girl and her mother are found in Alaska. Now the Pichelsteiner's become a family.

Kay, Mara
1
Masha
Day, 1968

A story of Russian life, based on the life of Catherine the Great.

Kay, Mara
2
Youngest Lady-in-Waiting
Day, 1971

This is the continuing story of Masha and the Grand Duchess, Alexandra of Russian royalty in the early 1800s.

Kendall, Carol
1
Gammage Cup
Harcourt, 1959

A group of Exiles, settle on a mountain top only to discover that their old enemies, the Mushrooms, are again fighting the Minnipins.

Kendall, Carol
2
Whisper of Glocken
Harcourt, 1965

The river is flooding. The Minnipins

try to find out why. The Hulks, a race of giants, built a dam. The Bell of Glocken tolled (whispered) and the dam collapsed.

Kerr, Judith
1
When Hitler Stole Pink Rabbit
Coward, 1971
A Jewish family weathers the experiences of being refugees in several countries during World War II. They expected to be gone for only a short time so Anna leaves her pink rabbit behind.

Kerr, Judith
2
Other Way Around
Coward, 1975
Anna and her family end up in England. They can't find work and are poor. Anna finds work and takes art lessons. Her brother, Max, goes on to Cambridge.

Kerr, Judith
3
Small Person Far Away
Coward, 1978
Anna marries a writer, Richard, and settles in England. She goes to Berlin to help her ill mother and learns more about her childhood and the feelings of Nazi survivors.

Key, Alexander
1
Escape to Witch Mountain
Westminster, 1968
Tia and Tony appear to be abandoned orphans but they are different from other children. But they see their mission and must follow their plans.

Key, Alexander
2
Return from Witch Mountain
Westminster, 1984
Tia and Tony are very concerned about the Planet Earth and their many Earth friends because of what might happen at the hands of an evil scientist and the power of greed.

Killilea, M.
1

Karen
Prentice Hall, 1952
Karen is the heroine in this book about the Killilea family.

Killilea, M.
2
With Love from Karen
Prentice Hall, 1952
Karen's older sister Gloria is featured in this book about the loveable Killilea family.

Kjelgaard, James
1
Big Red
Holiday, 1945
The story of a wonderful Irish Setter named Big Red and his owner who is the son of a trapper. He and Big Red grow up together.

Kjelgaard, James
2
Irish Red
Holiday, 1951
A story of one of Big Red's sons. He was the runt of the litter. Although he finally did win a dog show he was certainly a misfit for most of his young life.

Kjelgaard, James
3
Outlaw Red
Holiday, 1953
Sean, another son of Big Red, finds himself forced to survive in the wilderness.

Kjelgaard, James
A1
Snow Dog
Holiday, 1948
Link, a trapper, adds Queenie to his dog team only to lose her while she has a family. He finds one of her pups later in a trap. He releases him and trains him. The dog later saves his life.

Kjelgaard, James
A2
Wild Trek
Holiday, 1950
A trapper and his dog go into the mountains to rescue the pilot of a plane

that was downed with a famous naturalist aboard.

Knowles, John
1
Separate Peace
Macmillan, 1960
Gene and Finny are in Devon School in 1942 when Finney is injured because of Gene. They become close friends.

Knowles, John
2
Peace Breaks Out
HRW, 1981
Pete is back at Devon School; not as a student but as a teacher. The war is over and he wants peace and quiet. But tensions break out among the students.

Knudson, R. R.
1
Zanballer
Delacorte, 1972
Zan, a liberated girl, makes football history at school. She was encouraged to be a cheerleader, but instead forms a girls' football team.

Knudson, R. R.
2
Zanbanger
Harper, 1977
In this book Zan participates in basketball. The girls' team thinks she is too aggressive and the boys' team won't take her. She and Rinehart fight back by legal means.

Knudson, R. R.
3
Zanboomer
Harper, 1978
Zan is a winner on her high school baseball team but hurts her shoulder. She takes up cross-country running which is the first nonteam sport she has tried.

Knudson, R. R.
4
Zan Hagen's Marathon
Farrar, 1984
The sport is track as Zan tries to win a place on the U.S. Olympic team. She finds it is hard work and a great deal of pain.

Knudson, R. R.
5
Rinehart Lifts
Farrar, 1980
Zan helps her friend, Rinehart, lift weights. He would rather take care of his ferns but needs to fight for his rights as he is shunned by the Mighty Four.

Kruss, James
1
My Great-Grandfather and I
Atheneum, 1964
Boy's two sisters had the measles so he was to stay with great-grandfather who was a retired sailor and fisherman. For a whole week the two of them made up stories and poems about far away places.

Kruss, James
2
My Great-Grandfather,
the Heroes and I
Atheneum, 1973
Boy hurt his foot and couldn't go to school and his great-grandfather was too ill to move. So they both wrote stories about heroes to keep each other entertained. Soon everyone is involved.

Kruss, James
A1
Happy Islands Behind the Winds
Atheneum, 1966
Captain Madirankowitch of the Cicado beached on the Happy Islands during a storm. Plants and animals could understand each other. There were special parts of this island where everything is HAPPY.

Kruss, James
A2
Return to the Happy Islands
Atheneum, 1967
Captain Madirankowitch, who was shipwrecked on the Happy Island swore he would come back if he could. He was told it was possible but not guaranteed. There is no place like the Happy Islands.

Kruss, James
B1
Pauline and the Prince in the Wind
Atheneum, 1966
Pauline tells stories to the author in return for candy and other goodies. Her stories are all fantasies and she appears in most of them.

Kruss, James
B2
Letters to Pauline
Atheneum, 1971
This time the author tells Pauline the stories in exchange for supplies. She lives in Germany and he lives on Canary Island. His stories are non-sensical, fun and somewhat moralistic.

Kurtz, Katherine
A1
Camber of Culdi
Ballantine, 1976
A story about Camber and the king-dom of Gwyneed. He was the greatest of the Deryni, men with great mental powers. He must overthrow Imre and his sister.

Kurtz, Katherine
A2
Saint Camber
Ballantine, 1978
Camber was both a defender of humanity and a practitioner of Black Magic. He was loved and hated.

Kurtz, Katherine
A3
Camber the Heretic
Ballantine, 1981
The last of the "Legends of Camber of Culdi," the mystery man of medieval pageantry and magic. Even though he lost his son to the treachery of Imre he continues to fight for Gwyneed.

L'Engle, Madeleine
1
Wrinkle in Time
Farrar, 1962
Through a "wrinkle in time" an eerie midnight visitor leads three teenagers in search of a vanished scientist. They en-counter the terrors of the Tesseract.

L'Engle, Madeleine
2
Wind in the Door
Farrar, 1973
An alien creature, a dragon, is found in the garden. The story leads to the land of Mitochondrain and back home. Meg and Charles are again on another adventure.

L'Engle, Madeleine
3
Swiftly, Tilting Planet
Farrar, 1978
Charles travels through time and space, battling hard against an evil dictator. Charles is now 15 and Meg is married and expecting a baby, but she goes with him in spirit.

L'Engle, Madeleine
4
Many Waters
Farrar, 1986
The Murray twins, Dennys and Sandy are transported to a desert in Biblical times. A world as it existed before the flood. Noah is building his ark.

L'Engle, Madeleine
A1
Arm and the Starfish
Farrar, 1965
An excellent plot of tension and suspense stars Carol, Adam and the O'Keefes. Mystery surrounds the work at the laboratory and Adam, a marine biologist, is involved.

L'Engle, Madeleine
A2
Dragons in the Water
Farrar, 1976
Another taut, suspenseful novel with Polly and Charles O'Keefe. There is a murder aboard their freighter. They meet Simon whose life is threatened and Forsyth who is murdered.

L'Engle, Madeleine
A3
House Like a Lotus
Farrar, 1984
Polly travels to Cypress with Max, a wealthy and very talented artist.

L'Engle, Madeleine
B1
Meet the Austin's
Farrar, 1960

Maggy, an orphan, comes to live with the Austin's. She is not used to the ways of her new family and causes tension. Vicki and the rest of the family feels it but they come to love each other.

L'Engle, Madeleine
B2
Moon by Night
Farrar, 1963

A contemporary family story. Vicki is now two years older and meets a boy, Zachary, who has more family problems than she thinks she has. Her old friend, Andy, is more stable and reliable.

L'Engle, Madeleine
B3
Young Unicorns
Farrar, 1968

Vicki and the Austin's are involved in a plot to control men's minds by using a microlaser.

L'Engle, Madeleine
B4
Ring of Endless Light
Farrar, 1980

More adventures of Vicki, now 16, and the Austin family. She must cope with the death of her favorite grandparent and with her romantic involvements.

Ladd, Elizabeth
1
Meg of Heron's Neck
Morrow, 1961

Meg grows up on Heron's Neck and has the security of a stable family after being taken away from her free-living brother. At first she was resentful but soon learned to love her new life.

Ladd, Elizabeth
2
Mystery for Meg
Morrow, 1962

Meg, who likes to play detective, solves another mystery. She visits her brother on the island of Heron's Neck and they investigate a locked room in an old barn.

Ladd, Elizabeth
3
Meg's Mysterious Island
Morrow, 1963

Meg and her older brother, Allen, find money under the floor boards of an old barn. It was stolen money later taken from them by Hogton and Foxy.

Ladd, Elizabeth
4
Meg and Melissa
Morrow, 1964

Meg is a 13-year-old, scrappy babysitter for Melissa. She wonders about Melissa's past and why Melissa's guardians act so strange. Are her parents dead? Is she being hidden for a reason?

Ladd, Elizabeth
5
Trouble on Heron's Neck
Morrow, 1966

Meg goes off to look for a lost pet crow. What she finds is a fisherman and his daughter living on shore's edge. When she goes back again she finds intruders with guns.

Ladd, Elizabeth
6
Treasure on Heron's Neck
Morrow, 1967

Marty, with Meg and Kit, go treasure hunting in an old, supposedly abandoned, house.

Lampman, Evelyn
1
Shy Stegosaurus of Cricket Creek
Doubleday, 1955

A funny fantasy about a delightful dinosaur found by Joan and Joey who are twins. The dinosaur can speak English and he wants a friend.

Lampman, Evelyn
2
Shy Stegosaurus of Indian Springs
Doubleday, 1962

Another adventure with the supposedly extinct dinosaur. He lives near an Indian Reservation and helps an Indian boy, Huck, save his grandfather from being "modernized."

Langton, Jane
1
Her Majesty, Grace Jones
Harper, 1961
Grace convinces herself that she is the rightful heir to the throne of England. It is a way to get through the Great Depression.

Langton, Jane
2
Boyhood of Grace
Harper, 1972
A funny story about a girl with imagination of great magnitude. She wants the adventures she thinks only boys have. Her tomboy ways are disapproved of by family and friends.

Langton, Jane
A1
Diamond in the Window
Harper, 1962
Strange things happen to the Hall family's house. The diamond is only glass but as Edward and Eleanor watch the moonlight they have exciting adventures.

Langton, Jane
A2
Swing in the Summer House
Harper, 1967
Once again, the Hall family has exciting and terrifying adventures in their home. Edward and Eleanor go in the summer house against the signs reading otherwise.

Langston, Jane
A3
Astonishing Stereoscope
Harper, 1971
Magic is the base of Edward and Eleanor's new adventure. It lies in the stereoscope cards and teaches a lesson of how to cope with everyday happenings.

Langton, Jane
A4
Fledgling
Harper, 1980
In this fantasy, Georgie, a cousin of Edward and Eleanor, wants to fly. She makes friends with a Canadian goose and gets her wish.

Langton, Jane
A5
Fragile Flag
Harper, 1984
Georgie leads a children's march from Massachusetts to Washington, D.C., in protest of new, destructive missiles. She carries an old flag found in the attic.

Larom, Henry
1
Mountain Pony
McGraw-Hill, 1946
Andy gets a bronco and learns to love him. He takes good care of him but fears Garian, the horse thief and poacher.

Larom, Henry
2
Mountain Pony and the Pinto Colt
Wittlesey, 1947
Andy finds a pinto colt and uncovers a rustler's secret. He had spent the past year in the East attending school but found out about the rustlers on his return.

Larom, Henry
3
*Mountain Pony
and the Rodeo Mystery*
McGraw-Hill, 1949
Andy is in New York at the Madison Square Garden with the Rodeo. He has more adventure than he counted on when he discovers a mystery.

Larom, Henry
4
*Mountain Pony
and the Elkhorn Mystery*
McGraw-Hill, 1950
Andy and his horse discover a fire and another mystery. Andy inherited the

ranch and troublemakers think there is a treasure hidden there and start a forest fire.

Lawson, Robert
1
Rabbit Hill
Viking, 1944
All the animals living on the hill are concerned about the people moving into the big house but when they see "Please Drive Carefully on Account of Small Animals" they are satisfied.

Lawson, Robert
2
Tough Winter
Viking, 1954
All the animals on the hill suffer through a cold winter. Uncle Analdas said he knew it was coming and he was right.

Le Guin, Ursula
1
Wizard of Earthsea
Houghton, 1968
Ged, a young wizard, misuses his magical powers, allowing a terrible shadowbeast into the world. He is still in training and must hunt it down. He chases it throughout Earthsea.

Le Guin, Ursula
2
Tombs of Atuan
Atheneum, 1971
Ged needs to find the missing half of a magic ring, in the tombs of Atuan where Arha is being trained as a priestess. She must spend all her life there and Ged wants to free her.

Le Guin, Ursula
3
Farthest Shore
Atheneum, 1972
Ged must travel to the "Farthest Shore" and close the gap that is allowing darkness into the world. Arren, a young prince, goes with Ged on this mission. A battle between Good and Evil.

Leonard, Constance
1

Marina Mystery
Dodd, 1981
Tracy James and her boyfriend, Pete, love sailing and boats. But one day a body is found along side Tracy's boat and the mystery begins that involves Tracy in a dangerous way.

Leonard, Constance
2
Stowaway
Dodd, 1983
A marina mystery with Tracy and Pete set in the Bahamas. Tracy finds a stowaway, Tessa, in her cabin. She speaks no English and is kidnapped off the boat. Tracy, facing danger, rescues her.

Leonard, Constance
3
Aground
Dodd, 1984
A Tracy James mystery about mind control and runaway kids. Her friend's lobster business is threatened and she comes to his aid. What she finds is a cult and evil doings.

Lewis, C. S.
1
Lion, the Witch and the Wardrobe
Macmillan, 1950
Through the magic closet, Peter, Edmund, Susan and Lucy enter the fantastic land of Narnia, where the great lion, Asian, frees Narnia from the forever-winter spell of the White Winter.

Lewis, C. S.
2
Prince Caspian
Macmillan, 1951
Peter, Edmund, Susan and Lucy, with the help from Asian, assist good Prince Caspian in conquering the Telmarines and preserving the kingdom in Narnia.

Lewis, C. S.
3
Voyage of the "Dawn Treader"
Macmillan, 1952
Two of the children and their eccentric cousin, Eustace, help King Caspian

sail through magic waters to the End of the World in Narnia. Eustace is turned into a dragon.

Lewis, C. S.
4
Silver Chair
Macmillan, 1953
The children, with Asian's assistance, help Prince Rilian escape from the clutches of the magical silver chair in the Emerald Witch's underground kingdom.

Lewis, C. S.
5
Horse and His Boy
Macmillan, 1954
A talking horse and a boy prince save Narnia from invasion by Calormenes with the help of Asian and the children.

Lewis, C. S.
6
Magician's Nephew
Macmillan, 1955
Asian creates Narnia and gives the gift of speech to his animals. Because the land is good the Witch leaves. This is the basic information book about Narnia.

Lewis, C. S.
7
Last Battle
Macmillan, 1956
Jill and Eustace come to the aid of the young King Tirian in Narnia's last battle with the evil Calormenes, and their evil spirit, Tash.

Lewis, C. S.
A1
Out of the Silent Planet
Macmillan, 1938
Mr. Ransom is kidnapped by two friends. He is going to the Planet Mars where he observes the Earth from the Martian point of view.

Lewis, C. S.
A2
Perelandra
Macmillan, 1944
A planet, Venus, in a new space world

has been invaded by evil Dr. Weston. He is tempting the inhabitants, King and Lady. Dr. Ransom aids Lady to choose the path of perfection not corruption.

Lewis, C. S.
A3
That Hideous Strength
Macmillan, 1946
The story is set in England, and chronicles Satan's desire to dominate the world through evil magic and wizardry. Features Merlin the magician.

Lilius, Irmelin
1
Gold Crown Lane
Delacorte, 1969
There is death in the small town of Tulavail. The Halter children get involved in finding the killer in this mysterious crime-based death.

Lilius, Irmelin
2
Goldmaker's House
Delacorte, 1970
Bonadea learns that the owner of the big house in town is looking for a stone with which to make gold. This accounts for his peculiar behavior.

Lilius, Irmelin
3
Horse of the Night
Delacorte, 1971
The Halter children, with Bonadea have a special adventure when an explosion brings legendary horses back from the past. They also stop Mr. Klingkor from stealing the town's water for himself.

Lindgren, Astrid
1
Children of Noisy Village
Viking, 1962
Six children, three boys and three girls, live in Noisy Village. Each chapter is an episode in the lives of these energetic youngsters. Some about relatives, some about neighbors.

Lindgren, Astrid
2

Happy Times in Noisy Village
Viking, 1963
  Lisa, the teller of these happenings in the three adjoining villages in Sweden, captains about the liveliness and togetherness of of all the people living there.

Lindgren, Astrid
3
Christmas in Noisy Village
Viking, 1964
  Lisa tells about the traditional festivities of Noisy Village especially at Christmas time.

Lindgren, Astrid
4
Springtime in Noisy Village
Viking, 1966
  Lisa tells what children do in the spring, about the animals on the farm and the games children play.

Lindgren, Astrid
A1
Bill Bergson, Master Detective
Viking, 1952
  Bill, Anders and Eva-Lotta spend a wonderful summer putting on a circus show and inventing exciting games. Bill wants to become a real detective and shows a talent for observation and deduction.

Lindgren, Astrid
A2
Bill Bergson Lives Dangerously
Viking, 1954
  The summer is spent in pretend battles between the White Roses and the Red Roses until a real murder happened in their village. Bill has a chance to use his skill as a would-be detective.

Lindgren, Astrid
A3
Bill Bergson
and the White Rose Rescue
Viking, 1965
  Bill, Anders and Eva-Lotta are the White Roses and the "enemy" is Siten, Johnny and Benka of the Red Roses. This time the White Roses are involved in a kidnapping by enemy agents.

Lindgren, Astrid
B1
Emil in the Soup Tureen
Follett, 1970
  Emil lived with his parents and a sister, Ida. He was constantly in trouble. In this book he gets his head caught in a soup bowl and can't get it out. It took a lot of different events to do so.

Lindgren, Astrid
B2
Emil's Pranks
Follett, 1971
  Emil's pranks include locking himself in the tool chest three times in one day, catching a rat but caught his father's toe instead and accidentally spilling pudding on his father's head.

Lindgren, Astrid
B3
Emil and Piggy Beast
Follett, 1973
  Emil buys his sister a velvet-lined box at an auction. The box contains a letter with a valuable stamp. He has adventures with his pet pig.

Lingard, Joan
1
Twelfth Day of July
Nelson, 1970
  Sadie, a Protestant, and Kevin, a Catholic, living in Ireland, must face the consequences of their relationship.

Lingard, Joan
2
Across the Barricades
Nelson, 1972
  Sadie and Kevin cope with serious changes in their lives. They know their families are against their love and future plans.

Lingard, Joan
3
Into Exile
Nelson, 1973
  Sadie and Kevin are married. But, they are alone, isolated from their family and friends in Belfast and feel the pressure.

Lingard, Joan
4
Proper Place
Nelson, 1975

Sadie and Kevin have a baby and want to improve their life and their marriage so they move out of the city to a farm in Cheshire.

Lingard, Joan
5
Hostages to Fortune
Nelson, 1977

The farm Sadie and Kevin thought would make life better is sold and they must move again. Family opposition is still a problem in their lives.

Lingard, Joan
A1
Clearance
Nelson, 1974

The Ross family has had bad luck but Maggie endures. She expects a dull summer with her grandmother but when she makes friends with the visiting neighbors life becomes more interesting.

Lingard, Joan
A2
Resettling
Nelson, 1975

Another story of Maggie and her family. This time it is school, love and more family problems involved with moving to a new home and helping in her father's new business.

Lingard, Joan
A3
Pilgrimage
Nelson, 1976

Maggie and her boyfriend, James, take a trip during the summer and they learn more about each other than about the past they were seeking.

Lippincott, Joseph
1
Wilderness Champion
Lippincott, 1944

The story of Reddy, a champion hound who is adopted by a black wolf.

Lippincott, Joseph
2
Wolf King
Lippincott, 1949

A great wolf befriends Reddy, the hound. The friendship lasts even though Reddy is reclaimed and loved by his human owner.

Lipsyte, Robert
1
One Fat Summer
Harper, 1977

Bobby, an overweight 14-year-old, is hassled by a bully, by constant teasing and by his summer job. A funny, touching story of growing up in the '50s.

Lipsyte, Robert
2
Summer Rules
Harper, 1981

Bobby, now 16, is a camp counselor with some responsibility, and less hassled by others. He meets a girl, Sheila, and finds out how complicated growing up can be.

Lipsyte, Robert
3
Summerboy
Harper, 1982

Bobby is now 18. His quest is girls, love and glory. He works summers in a laundry, and fights for the betterment of life for those who live at Lake Rumson all year 'round.

Little, Jean
1
Look Through My Window
Harper, 1970

The story of a friendship between two girls, Emily and Kate. Emily is an only child and doesn't want her four cousins to come and live with her but she soon becomes close to all the children.

Little, Jean
2
Kate
Harper, 1971

This is a story of Kate from *Look Through My Window*. She and Emily are still friends and Kate is in need of friends as she and her family are having problems.

Little, Jean
A1
Mine For Keeps
Little, 1962

Sally is crippled. She has a puppy named Susie who is a great companion and help during difficult times. Sally starts to attend regular school.

Little, Jean
A2
Spring Begins in March
Little, 1964

Meg is Sally's younger sister. She is an underachiever at school and has problems at home because the room she wanted for her own was taken over by Grandma.

Little, Jean
B1
From Anna
Harper, 1972

Anna and her family move from Germany to Canada. She is slowly losing her eyesight.

Little, Jean
B2
Listen for the Singing
Dutton, 1977

It is five years later and Anna is in regular high school after spending a whole year in Sight School. Her brother has been blinded and she can relate to how he feels.

Lofting, Hugh
1
Story of Dr. Dolittle
Lippincott, 1920/1948/1988

Dr. Dolittle is a very kind doctor who is fond of animals. He understands their language. He and some of his friendly animals go to Africa to cure the monkeys of a strange sickness.

Lofting, Hugh
2
Voyage of Dr. Dolittle
Lippincott, 1923/1950/1968

This time Dr. Dolittle goes to Spider-

monkey Island. He spent a lot of time learning the language of the animals.

Lofting, Hugh
3
Dr. Dolittle's Caravan
Delacorte, 1924/1954/1988

Dr. Dolittle takes his circus to London and with the help of Pippinella, the green canary who was not supposed to be able to sing, he stages a bird opera which took London by storm.

Lofting, Hugh
4
Dr. Dolittle's Circus
Delacorte, 1924/1988

His circus is a success because of Pushmi-pullyu. But that is only the beginning of a very special circus.

Lofting, Hugh
5
Dr. Dolittle's Zoo
Lippincott, 1925

Dr. Dolittle establishes a wonderful zoo at Puddleby. The best possible accommodations are there for all the animals.

Lofting, Hugh
6
Dr. Dolittle on the Moon
Lippincott, 1928/1988

Dr. Dolittle goes to the moon on the back of a giant moth. Chee Chee, the monkey, and others go with him. On the moon they encounter some strange vegetable life.

Lofting, Hugh
7
Dr. Dolittle's Return
Lippincott, 1933

Dr. Dolittle is finally going to come back. He is eagerly awaited by his friends. He arrives on an enormous locust.

Lofting, Hugh
8
Dr. Dolittle and the Secret Lake
Lippincott, 1948

Mudface, an old turtle who lived during Noah's time, is rescued by Dr.

Dolittle. He was dug out of the bottom of a lake where he was buried due to an earthquake.

Lofting, Hugh
9
Dr. Dolittle and the Green Canary
Lippincott, 1950/1988
Pippinella, the green canary, is a good friend of Dr. Dolittle. This story is about her life before joining the Dr. and her search for her lost master and some mysterious stolen papers.

Lofting, Hugh
10
Dr. Dolittle's Post Office
Lippincott, 1951/1988
Dr. Dolittle discovers animal writing in addition to their language. So he started a mail service for animals and birds. It is called the Swallow Mail.

Lofting, Hugh
11
Dr. Dolittle's Garden
Lippincott, 1955/1988
This book has many tales about the creatures that live in Dr. Dolittle's garden, especially the insects. Dr. Dolittle learns about the giant moths and their language.

Lovelace, Maud
1
Betsy-Tacy and Tib
Crowell, 1941
Three young girls who like each other have mischievous fun. They try hard to be good girls but everything they do together turns out bad.

Lovelace, Maud
2
Betsy and Tacy Go over the Big Hill
Crowell, 1942
Tacy and Betsy are older and travel father from home. They meet an immigrant girl, Naifi, and have a wonderful experience.

Lovelace, Maud
3
Betsy and Tacy Go Downtown
Crowell, 1943

Betsy, Tacy and Tib explore their neighborhood. They find the library, the local hotel and also go to a theatre.

Lovelace, Maud
4
Heavens to Betsy
Crowell, 1945
This is the story of Betsy's first year in high school.

Lovelace, Maud
5
Betsy in Spite of Herself
Crowell, 1946
Betsy is now a sophomore in high school but still has her old friends from childhood.

Lovelace, Maud
6
Betsy Was a Junior
Crowell, 1947
Betsy is a junior at Deep Valley High. She attends football games, has boyfriends and decides she wants to stay with her friends and not join an exclusive sorority.

Lovelace, Maud
7
Betsy and Joe
Crowell, 1948
This is Betsy's senior year at Deep Valley High. She reflects on her early life and decides she is happy with herself and her family. And of course, with Joe.

Lovelace, Maud
8
Betsy and the Great World
Crowell, 1952
Betsy travels to Europe without her family. She enjoys everything she sees and does all she can to see everything. She has a bit of romance, too.

Lovelace, Maud
9
Betsy's Wedding
Crowell, 1947
Betsy marries her childhood sweetheart, Joe.

Lowry, Lois
1

Anastasia Krupnik
Houghton, 1979
Anastasia has trouble with her teachers, her parents, her grandmother, etc., etc., etc. She is apprehensive about having a baby brother to add to her problems.

Lowry, Lois
2
Anastasia Again
Houghton, 1981
Two years later, Anastasia add boys to her long list of troubles. One is her obviously bright younger brother. She is two years older (12) and may have to make still another adjustment.

Lowry, Lois
3
Anastasia at Your Service
Houghton, 1982
Anastasia looks at a long boring summer until she becomes involved with Mrs. Bellingham. She works as a maid, which she dislikes but can't quit.

Lowry, Lois
4
Anastasia, Ask Your Analyst
Houghton, 1984
Anastasia's three-year-old brother, Sam, aids her with her science project. But she is still frustrated and blames her family for her mixed-up life. She talks out her problems.

Lowry, Lois
5
Anastasia on Her Own
Houghton, 1985
Anastasia tries to run the household while her mother is out of town. She has an organization schedule to make things easy.

Lowry, Lois
6
Anastasia Has the Answers
Houghton, 1986
Anastasia plays cupid for her widowed uncle and also has a "romance" of her own: a crush on her gym teacher.

Lowry, Lois
7

Anastasia's Chosen Career
Houghton, 1987
Anastasia is quite mature and tries to take a modeling course but becomes involved in a book store.

Lowry, Lois
8
All About Sam
Houghton, 1988
Anastasia's baby brother Sam, tells his story from birth to now (pre-school). It is a trial trying to fit into the Krupnik family. He like Anastasia but . . .

Lowry, Lois
A1
One Hundreth Thing About Caroline
Houghton, 1983
Caroline's mother dates a man in the same building. She finds he must "eliminate the children." Caroline and J.P., her brother, figure that must be them! They find out he is an author.

Lowry, Lois
A2
Switcharound
Houghton, 1985
Caroline, 11 and J.P., 13 spend their summer with their father and his new family. He places a lot of responsibility on them. They don't like it and seek revenge.

MacGregor, Ellen
1
Miss Pickerell Goes to Mars
McGraw-Hill, 1951
Miss Pickerell is accidently stowed away on a ship bound for Mars. She is not welcome by the crew.

MacGregor, Ellen
2
Miss Pickerell Goes Underseas
McGraw-Hill, 1953
Miss Pickerell puts on a diver's suit and goes underwater to recover her famous red rock collection from Mars.

MacGregor, Ellen
3
Miss Pickerell and the Geiger Counter
McGraw-Hill, 1953

Miss Pickerell takes her pet cow to the veterinarian. She finds herself substituting for the sheriff and somehow discovers uranium.

MacGregor, Ellen
4
Miss Pickerell Goes to the Arctic
McGraw-Hill, 1954
Miss Pickerell flies to the Arctic to rescue a downed plane. She is downed herself and must be rescued along with the other plane survivors.

MacGregor, Ellen
5
Miss Pickerell on the Moon
McGraw-Hill, 1965
Miss Pickerell's cow (and her cat) have fallen ill from an epidemic of unknown germs. There is no treatment so she goes to the moon to look for some molds that are needed.

MacGregor, Ellen
6
Miss Pickerell Goes on a Dig
McGraw-Hill, 1966
Miss Pickerell goes on an archeological excavation to unearth some history before the road department comes along and digs everything up as they widen the road.

MacGregor, Ellen
7
Miss Pickerell Harvests the Sea
McGraw-Hill, 1968
Miss Pickerell helps a friend who has an ocean farm. She doesn't understand at first but learns a great deal about oceanography.

MacGregor, Ellen
8
Miss Pickerell
and the Weather Satellite
McGraw-Hill, 1971
Miss Pickerell learns a lot about modern technology at the weather station. She prevents a flood by using laser beams and space stations.

MacGregor, Ellen
9

Miss Pickerell Meets Mr. H.U.M.
McGraw-Hill, 1974
While trying to think of a name for her cow, the telephone rings and a chain of events started. It was all very upsetting. H.U.M. is a computer that's going to take over the world.

MacGregor, Ellen
10
Miss Pickerell
Takes the Bull by the Horns
McGraw-Hill, 1976
Miss Pickerell is dead set against cloning. There is a bill in Congress and she does her civic duty with letters and a protest march.

MacGregor, Ellen
11
Miss Pickerell and the Supertanker
McGraw-Hill, 1978
Miss Pickerell plugs a leak in a tanker and feeds oil-eating microbes.

MacGregor, Ellen
12
Miss Pickerell
Tackles the Energy Crisis
McGraw-Hill, 1980
Miss Pickerell's trip to the long-awaited Fair is cancelled. There is a fuel shortage because of an earthquake and the Fair must be postponed. She gets a formula for ethanol.

MacGregor, Ellen
13
Miss Pickerell and the Blue Whales
McGraw-Hill, 1983
Miss Pickerell organizes a boycott to save the Blue Whales from harpoonists.

MacKellar, William
1
Secret of the Dark Tower
McKay, 1967
When some diamonds are found, "accidents" begin to happen, and one night a threatening note draws two boys to a deserted castle.

MacKellar, William
2
Secret of the Sacred Stone

McKay, 1970

Two young boys end up smack in the middle of a daring Scottish Nationalist plot.

Manes, Stephen
1
That Game from Outer Space
Dutton, 1983

Oscar finds himself involved in an unusual adventure with aliens from outer space. These aliens need their rocket repaired. A video game to end all video games.

Manes, Stephen
2
Oscar J. Noodleman's Television Network
Dutton, 1984

When Oscar gets a home video recorder, a mystery begins.

Manes, Stephen
3
Chicken Trek: Third Strange Thing that Happened to Noodleman
Dutton, 1987

Two hundred eleven chicken franchises! And a mad scientist? Oscar is really into it now. Cousin Prechtwinkle turned a picklemobile into a Rem Dem to disappear and reappear at will.

Mayhar, A.
1
Lords of the Triple Moon
Atheneum, 1984

The House of Enthala is destroyed, and all that remains are two small, helpless children.

Mayhar, A.
2
Runes of the Lyre
Atheneum, 1982

A magic Lyre is the key to salvation for the people of Hasyih when they are threatened by a group of rebels awakening in a neighboring world.

Mayhar, A.
3
Soul Singer of Tyrnos
Atheneum, 1981

Yeleeve can sing the image of a soul on the wall to see what is there, good or evil. She is from the Tyrnos school for singers. This ability can be misused.

Mazer, Harry
1
Dollar Man
Delacorte, 1974

Marcus, a fat 14-year-old boy, feels that he must find his real father in order to establish his own identity. The confrontation is not what he had imagined.

Mazer, Harry
2
I Love You, Stupid
Crowell, 1981

Marcus is now 17 and considers himself an adult. He has an old friend, Wendy, and a new friend who becomes a love.

McCaffrey, Anne
1
Dragonflight
Ballantine, 1968

Great dragons of Pern sweep through the skies to fight off the invasion of space spores during Threadfall.

McCaffrey, Anne
2
Dragonquest
Ballantine, 1971

Pern needs its dragons and dragonriders in order to survive. They have formed a telepathic bond with man. Periodically Threadfall occurs and it takes cooperation to survive.

McCaffrey, Anne
3
White Dragon
Ballantine, 1978

Ruth, a pure white dragon, and Jaxon, find themselves in danger but must prevent a big disaster.

McCaffrey, Anne
PrA1
Moreta, Dragonlady of Pern
Ballantine, 1983

This is a book about other heroines who lived on Pern in earlier times.

McCaffrey, Anne
A1
Dragonsong
Atheneum, 1976
On the Planet Pern, forbidden by her father to indulge in music in any way because it is a career only for men. Menolly runs away to a life with the dragons and fights the enemy "Threads."

McCaffrey, Anne
A2
Dragonsinger
Atheneum, 1977
Menolly, now living with the Fire Dragons, learns a great deal about music and its role in Pern. And the role of girls.

McCaffrey, Anne
A3
Dragondrums
Atheneum, 1979
Pern is in danger, but Piemur will outwit Threadfall and win the fire-lizard of his dreams.

McCaffrey, Anne
B1
Crystal Singer
Doubleday, 1982
Killashandra has perfect pitch and wants to sing but is prevented from doing so. In Ballybran she could succeed but she would have to make many serious sacrifices to qualify.

McCaffrey, Anne
B2
Killashandra
Ballantine, 1985
Killashandra has great musical talents but because of the control of this field by the leaders she cannot pursue her career as she would like.

McCloskey, Robert
1
Homer Price
Viking, 1943
Six tales which acquaint the reader with Homer Price. The most well-known is the doughnut episode but there are others.

McCloskey, Robert
2
Centerburg Tales
Viking, 1951
Further adventures of Homer Price and reminiscences of his Grandpa Hercules: weeds that cover the town and a jukebox that plays music everyone dances to; all because of a mad scientist.

McHugh, Elizabeth
1
Raising a Mother Isn't Easy
Greenwillow, 1983
Karen, a Korean, is adopted by a single woman. Karen tries to find her new Mom a husband.

McHugh, Elizabeth
2
Karen's Sister
Greenwillow, 1983
Karen's mother adopts a second Korean child, and finds a husband with three children of his own.

McHugh, Elizabeth
3
Karen and Vicki
Greenwillow, 1984
Karen learns to live with a whole family, including stepsister, Vicki.

McInerney, Judith
1
Judge Benjamin, Superdog
Holiday, 1982
A funny story about a St. Bernard. He gets his "human family" in and out of disaster after disaster. It is told from his point of view.

McInerney, Judith
2
Judge Benjamin, Superdog Secret
Holiday, 1983
Judge Benjamin, weighing about 200 pounds, stows away in his "human" family's camper for a three-week vacation.

McInerney, Judith
3
Judge Benjamin, Superdog Rescue
Holiday, 1984

Gramps regrets his decision to allow Judge Benjamin to move in and run things on his farm.

McInerney, Judith
4
Judge Benjamin, Superdog Surprise
Holiday, 1985
Judge Benjamin takes care of his "human" family and also helps a neighbor during a blizzard.

McInerney, Judith
5
Judge Benjamin, Superdog Gift
Holiday, 1986
Loretta, an elderly friend, collapses on the sidewalk and Judge Benjamin and his new mate, Agatha, rescue her. When she disappears from the hospital Agatha must find her again.

McKillip, Patricia
1
Moon-Flash
Atheneum, 1984
Kyreol and Terje begin their adventures in other worlds.

McKillip, Patricia
2
Moon and the Face
Atheneum, 1985
Kyreol's mission to another planet and Terje's trip to observe their old river home, bring both of them unexpected dangers.

McKillip, Patricia
A1
Riddle Master of Hed
Atheneum, 1976
Morgon, the prince of Hed, tries to find the meaning of the three stars that are on his harp, and imprinted on his head.

McKillip, Patricia
A2
Heir of Sea and Fire
Atheneum, 1977
When Morgon fails to return from his quest, three people set out to find him, including his fiancée, Raederle. She meets up with the shape-changers.

McKillip, Patricia
A3
Harpist in the Wind
Atheneum, 1979
In the midst of conflict, the Prince of Hed, Morgon, and his friend, Raederle, learns to harp the wind and finds out who the shape-changers are.

McKinley, Robin
1
Hero and the Crown
Atheneum, 1984
Another fantasy about witches, dragons and princesses. With the help of Luthe and the Blue Sword, Aerin establishes herself as the daughter of the Damarian King. A prequel to Blue Sword.

McKinley, Robin
2
Blue Sword
Atheneum, 1982
Harry, bored with her sheltered life, goes to Istan, but wants to see where the Free Hillfolk live. She discovers magic in herself when she is kidnapped by a king with mysterious powers.

McLean, Allan
1
Ribbon of Fire
Harcourt, 1963
Alasdair and the Skye crofters try to hold on to their land in 1885. A vivid tale of oppression and its tragic results.

McLean, Allan
2
Sound of Trumpets
Harcourt, 1967
Alasdair, oppressed in his own land, leaves for America. He and Lachiann lead a partisan fight but are beaten.

McNeill, Janet
1
Battle of St. George Without
Little, 1968
Matt McGinley's playhouse, a church, is threatened by a sinister gang.

McNeill, Janet
2

Goodby, Dove Square
Little, 1969

Matt and his friends go back to their old neighborhood and find out one of their old friends, Shaky Trick, is living in a house that is about to be demolished.

Miller, Frances
1
Truth Trap
Dutton, 1980

Matt runs away with his deaf sister because his parents have been killed and he doesn't want to go to an orphanage. He lies to protect them both but she is killed and he is blamed.

Miller, Frances
2
Aren't You the One Who . . .
Atheneum, 1983

Matt is cleared of the death of his sister and finds a friend in Lieutenant Ryder. He still has to live with his past and tries to hide from the world.

Milne, A. A.
1
Winnie the Pooh
Dutton, 1926

Christopher Robin joins Pooh and others in adventurous exploits. Each chapter is a different story about the many friends of Robin: Piglet, Eeyore, Kanga, Roo and others.

Milne, A. A.
2
House at Pooh Corner
Dutton, 1928

More about Robin, Pooh and others, including Tigger.

Montgomery, Lucy
1
Emily of the New Moon
Bantam, 1986

Emily, an orphan, moves to New Moon Farm. A story like Anne of Green Gables.

Montgomery, Lucy
2
Emily Climbs
Bantam, 1986

Emily wants to be a writer. She leaves home to attend school, and learns of life.

Montgomery, Lucy
3
Emily's Quest
Bantam, 1982

Emily is grown up and faces life much in the same vein as Anne.

Montgomery, Lucy
A1
Anne of Green Gables
Putnam, 1935

Anne is a skinny girl with red hair and freckles. She is very high-spirited and mischievous. This the first in a long series about a likeable girl and her friends.

Montgomery, Lucy
A2
Anne of Avanlea
Grosset, 1936

Sixteen-year-old Anne is teaching school, but has not yet matured enough to control her high spirits.

Montgomery, Lucy
A3
Anne of the Islands
Grosset, 1915

Anne, now in college, finds romance. She must plan for her future, perhaps away from home. But marriage is pending.

Montgomery, Lucy
A4
Anne of Windy Poplars
Grosset, 1936

Anne gets her first job away from Green Gables and works for the proud and intolerant Pringle family. In Summerside there are both supporters and detractors of this controversial family.

Montgomery, Lucy
A5
Anne's House of Dreams
Grosset, 1917

It is Anne's wedding day. She and Gilbert will be married at Green Gables, outdoors in the orchard. It is an outstanding wedding. Then Anne goes home to her white house.

Montgomery, Lucy
A6
Anne of Ingleside
Grosset, 1939
Anne and Gilbert have five children. In this story she goes back to Avonlea to visit and recalls all the happy times she had and all the lovely friends she made.

Montgomery, Lucy
A7
Rainbow Valley
Bantam, 1985
Rainbow Valley is a special place for Anne's children to play. They meet the Meredith children and have lots of wonderful adventures.

Montgomery, Lucy
A8
Rilla of Ingleside
Bantam, 1985
Rilla is Anne's youngest daughter. She is 14 and dreams about her first date and first kiss. But the war comes and Rilla's life, like everyone else's, is changed.

Montgomery, Lucy
B1
Chronicles of Avonlea
Grosset, 1940
This is a book about the people and places on Prince Edward Island. It gives meaning to the Anne books by bringing alive the atmosphere of the setting.

Montgomery, Lucy
B2
Further Chronicles of Avonlea
Grosset, 1953
A more intimate look at Avonlea and the place where Anne lived, grew up, went to school, made friends, etc. All the people come alive as they relate to Anne.

Moon, Sheila
1
Knee-Deep in Thunder
Atheneum, 1967
Maris begins a long, hard journey of terrors and beauties when she picks up

a stone in a cave. She meets talking animals and befriends beetles, ants, mice, etc.

Moon, Sheila
2
Hunt down the Prize
Atheneum, 1971
Maris and her new animal friends have to capture some monsters before the monsters hurt someone, especially on Halloween.

Morgan, Alison
1
All Kinds of Prickles
Nelson, 1980
Paul lives with his grandfather and has a pet goat. His grandfather dies and he must go live with Aunt Jean. He is afraid he will have to give up his goat, Davy.

Morgan, Alison
2
Paul's Kite
Atheneum, 1981
Paul, now living with his missing mother, amuses himself by visiting all of the London place names on his Monopoly board, until a violent accident happens.

Mowat, Farley
1
Lost in the Barrens
Little, 1956
Stranded in the Canadian wilderness, a teenager and his Indian friend find that good sense, cooperation and patience can mean survival.

Mowat, Farley
2
Curse of the Viking Grave
Little, 1966
Three boys and a girl in search of Viking relics meet Eskimo and Indian tribes. Awasin, Jamie and Peetyuk learn a great deal about survival in the cold of Northern Canada.

Murphy, Shirley
A1
Nightpool

Harper, 1985

Tebriel is injured in battle with the Dark Raiders of Tirror. He is healed by talking otters and sets out to fight again.

Murphy, Shirley
A2
Ivory Lyre
Harper, 1987

With the help of four dragons Tebriel and Kiri rise against the Dark Raiders and locate the magical Ivory Lyre. But not before they are captured and tortured.

Murphy, Shirley
A3
Dragonbards
Harper, 1988

Prince Tebriel and his friends fight against the Dark Raider that threatens them. He must go through the Castle of Doors and face what he might find there.

Murphy, Shirley
B1
Ring of Fire
Atheneum, 1977

Because of their occult powers Thorn and Zephy of Ere know about death and the future but a greater evil appears. They must rescue others like themselves from the oppressor of Burgdeeth.

Murphy, Shirley
B2
Wolf Bell
Atheneum, 1979

With the help of wolves, Jerthon and Ramad search for the Runestone to save their planet, Ere.

Murphy, Shirley
B3
Castle of Hape
Atheneum, 1980

Ramad searches for Luff Eresi because he needs their help in ridding Ere of the negative powers of Hape, the evil monster. They can cloud the minds of the Seers of Carriol: half men, half horses.

Murphy, Shirley
B4

Caves of Fire and Ice
Atheneum, 1980

Again with the help of the wolves, Skeelie and Ramad aid Ere. Ramad is separated from his friend Telien, as she fulfills a fate of her own.

Namioka, Lensey
1
Samurai and Long-Nosed Devils
McKay, 1976

Zenta and Matsuzo are samurai without a master. Zenta's friend, Hambei, helps hire them as bodyguards. There the adventure begins.

Namioka, Lensey
2
White Serpent Castle
McKay, 1976

During the struggle for a warlord's territory, Zenta and Matsuzo, the two samurai, attempt to secure power for the rightful heir.

Namioka, Lensey
3
Valley of the Broken Cherry Trees
Delacorte, 1980

Someone is damaging the sacred cherry trees and Zenta and Matsuzo become involved in the mystery.

Namioka, Lensey
4
Village of the Vampire Cat
Delacorte, 1981

When Zenta and Matsuzo return to the village of their former teacher, they find that it is being terrorized by a mysterious killer.

Nash, Mary
1
While Mrs. Coverlet Was Away
Little, 1958

Toad's father is away and the housekeeper has been called home. Toad, his brother, Malcolm, and his sister, Molly, manage very well and learn about making money.

Nash, Mary
2
Mrs. Coverlet's Magicians

Little, 1961

Again the housekeeper is away at a bake-off. Toad uses his witchcraft set to get rid of the babysitter.

Naylor, Mary

3

Mrs. Coverlet's Detectives

Little, 1965

The three Persever children go to New York to find a valuable tortoise shell cat, Nervous, that was reported missing after the cat show.

Naylor, P. R.

1

Shadows on the Wall

Atheneum, 1980

While in England, Dan feels strange as he approaches some ancient landmarks. He is caught in a time change that takes him back to the time of the Black Death.

Naylor, P. R.

2

Faces in the Water

Atheneum, 1981

Daniel spends the summer with his grandmother in York, PENNSYLVANIA and people and events from York, ENGLAND seem to appear, disappear and reappear.

Naylor, P. R.

3

Footprints at the Window

Atheneum, 1981

Dan and his gypsy friends move among superstitious people and are frightened by the supernatural atmosphere. Dan is a descendant of a Faw gypsy.

Naylor, P. R.

A1

Witch's Sister

Atheneum, 1975

Lynn thinks her sister is learning witchcraft from a neighbor and is convinced on the weekend she and her sister are left in her care.

Naylor, P. R.

A2

Witch Water

Atheneum, 1977

Lynn knows that Mrs. Tuggle is involved in witchcraft but can't convince anyone of her evil.

Naylor, P. R.

A3

Witch Herself

Atheneum, 1978

Lynn and Mouse look into Mrs. Tuggle's past to see if they can prove she is a witch.

Naylor, P. R.

B1

Agony of Alice

Atheneum, 1985

Alice is a motherless teenager. Her friends are Pamela and Elizabeth. She wants Miss Cole for a teacher but gets Mrs. Plotkin. At the end she realizes this was for the best.

Naylor, P. R.

B2

Alice in Rapture, Sort of

Atheneum, 1989

Alice and Patrick are dating and in love. She wonders about the effects of kissing and decides they should be friends. Alice, Elizabeth and Pamela have a secret pact to find a boyfriend.

Nesbit, Edith

1

Story of the Treasure Seekers

Ernest Benn, 1899

The Bastable children can see the family and their house going downhill since the death of their mother. They hold a meeting and decide to raise the needed money.

Nesbit, Edith

2

Wouldbegoods

Ernest Benn, 1901

The Bastable children want to do something nice for someone everyday but these good intentions sometimes go awry.

Nesbit, Edith

3

New Treasurer Seekers
Coward, 1904

Since they were successful at their own fund-raising exploits the Bastable children decide to hunt treasure for others.

Ney, John
1
Ox, the Story of the Kid at the Top
Little, 1970

Ox is a very rich boy who lives an unconventional life with his fast swinging parents. His father rents a helicopter to look at cows for Ox's book report. (They looked at steers, not cows).

Ney, John
2
Ox Goes North
Harper, 1973

Ox goes to summer camp in Vermont. He is now 15 and finds life in the camp not to his liking. He is more used to "life in the fast lane."

Ney, John
3
Ox Under Pressure
Lippincott, 1976

Ox, now 17, is having some serious thoughts about his future and the past wild life he has led.

Ney, John
4
Ox and the Prime-Time Kid
Pineapple, 1985

Ox, 17, helps another mixed-up kid look for his mother.

Nixon, Joan
1
Family Apart
Bantam, 1987

Orphans from the East were being sent to the Midwest for adoption and farm work. Although Frances, Megan, Mike, Danny, Peg and Petey were not orphans their mother sent them for a better life.

Nixon, Joan
2
Caught in the Act

Bantam, 1988

The six Kelly children were placed in adoptive homes in Missouri. The first book was about Frances and Petey and this one is about Mike whose life is not as happy as the other children.

Nixon, Joan
3
In the Face of Danger
Bantam, 1988

This is another episode in the lives of the six Kelly children. It includes more about Megan, Danny and Peg but covers the other children, too. Some are happy and satisfied and others are not.

Nixon, Joan
4
Place to Belong
Bantam, 1989

This is the final book of this Orphan Train Quartet and the six Kelly children. Each book covered one orphan's touching story of the people who adopted them and their adjustment to it.

Nixon, Joan
A1
Maggie, Too
Harcourt, 1985

Margaret is sent to live with her unknown Grandma for the summer. She resents going but finds that the busy family, her active Grandma and neighbor activities make her rethink her decisions.

Nixon, Joan
A2
And Maggie Makes Three
Harcourt, 1986

Maggie is happy living with her grandmother. She becomes an actress in a school musical, made good friends and has adjusted to her father's marriage to a girl half his age.

Nixon, Joan
A3
Maggie Forevermore
Harcourt, 1987

Maggie was to spend Christmas with her Grandma and her friends. Instead her father wanted her to come to

California with him and his new wife. She didn't want to go but had a surprising good time.

Norton, André
1
Crystal Gryphon
Atheneum, 1972
Kerovan and his bride journey to the farthest reaches of the wilderness to save their people.

Norton, André
2
Jargon Pard
Atheneum, 1974
Kerovan had his birthright tampered with, but he is given a magical belt.

Norton, André
3
Gryphon in Glory
Atheneum, 1984
Kerovan is journeying on a secret mission in the Waste where the evil powers of the Dark threaten at every hand. Joisan, his wife, sets out to look for him.

Norton, André
4
Gryphon's Eyrie
Atheneum, 1984
This is the final book of Kerovan and Joisan as they fight and conquer the Dark evil.

Norton, André
A1
Rebel Spurs
World, 1962
Drew thinks his father is dead, that he was killed during the Civil War. But he finds out that he is still alive and living in the West.

Norton, André
A2
Ride, Proud Rebel
World, 1961
Hunt, Drew's father, was a legend in Arizona. He had control of ranches and horses. Drew finds him but does not reveal who he is until he learns more about the man. What he learns is surprising.

Norton, André
B1
Moon of Three Rings
Viking, 1966
The Free Traders of the future fight to save the galaxy from domination.

Norton, André
B2
Exiles of the Stars
Viking, 1971
While on a mission for the Thothan priests, the Free Trader's ship is forced down on a barren planet, seemingly unhabited but a preserved alien race is seeking new bodies.

Norton, André
C1
Stars Are Ours
World, 1954
This is another of Norton's science fiction stories about the strength of man's desire to be free. There are heroic deeds and improbable situations.

Norton, André
C2
Star Born
World, 1957
Underground passages are the secret to man's success in this follow-up story of man's quest for personal liberty.

Norton, André
D1
Zero Stone
Viking, 1968
Murdoc's Zero Stone ring, which he inherited from his father, has secret powers. It will help Murdoc find out information about Eet, the feline mutant.

Norton, André
D2
Uncharted Stars
Viking, 1969
Murdoc continues to search for the Zero Stone, the secret of his legacy, but he first must find the map he needs. He, Jern and Eet, the mutant, look for it.

Norton, André
D3
Year of the Unicorn

Viking, 1965

Murdoc searches for the Zero stone seeking the map he needs. It will also clear up Eet's feline origin.

Norton, André
E1
Star Ka'at
World, 1976

Two stray cats, Tiro and Mer, communicate with two children, orphan Jim and poor, Black Elly, and tell them they are from another planet and then take them there.

Norton, André
E2
Star Ka'at's World
Walker, 1978

Elly and Jim travel with the cats to their planet and are kept as partial prisoners because they cannot learn ESP. They run away.

Norton, André
E3
Star Ka'at and the Plant People
Walker, 1979

Elly and Jim rescue a group of plant people, who produce metal and become deeply involved with the super cat race.

Norton, André
E4
Star Ka'ats and the Winged Warriors
Walker, 1981

Magical rays cause insects to get larger and larger on the planet where Jim and Elly Mae are staying. They must be controlled before they destroy other colonies.

Norton, André
F1
Judgement on Janus
Harcourt, 1963

Another Norton fantasy about the known and unknown ingredients of other worlds. We meet the Ifts and the great evil that endangers them. Ayyar and his friends will fight that evil.

Norton, André
F2

Victory on Janus
Harcourt, 1966

Ayyar and his friend awaken from their long sleep. The evil force has risen again and wants to get rid of the Ifts. The battle takes place in the Waste.

Norton, Mary
1
Borrowers
Harcourt, 1952

A world where the people are no taller than a pencil. They hide under the floorboards and live on things borrowed from the people who live above them.

Norton, Mary
2
Borrowers Afield
Harcourt, 1955

The Borrowers escape capture in the house but now have to live in the field when there is constant danger.

Norton, Mary
3
Borrowers Afloat
Harcourt, 1959

The Borrowers must move again. This time downstream in a teakettle. Pod, Homily and Arrietty have narrow escapes when a flood sweeps them along.

Norton, Mary
4
Borrowers Aloft
Harcourt, 1961

This story tells how Pod, Homily and Arrietty plan their escape from the attic of Mr. and Mrs. Platter. They learn about balloons and now live in a rectory.

Norton, Mary
5
Borrowers Avenged
Harcourt, 1982

The Borrowers set up house in an old rectory. They must avoid being seen by any humans but they need the things humans supply.

Norton, Mary
6

Poor Stainless
Harcourt, 1971
  Homily tells Arrietty about a narrow escape from humans when her cousin, Stainess, was missing and had to be found.

O'Brien, John
1
Silver Chief, Dog of the North
Winston, 1933
  Jim Thorne of the Canadian Royal Mounted Police trains a dog to help him in his work. The dog is Silver Chief and he becomes invaluable to Jim.

O'Brien, John
2
Silver Chief to the Rescue
Winston, 1937
  In the snowbound North a doctor is fighting an epidemic of diptheria among the natives. Jim Thorne and his dog team, led by Silver Chief, bring the necessary serum just in time.

O'Brien, John
3
Return of Silver Chief
Winston, 1943
  Jim Thorne of the Mounties and his dog Silver Chief look for an escaped Nazi prisoner.

O'Brien, John
4
Royal Red
Winston, 1951
  Mr. McKinnon wants to exploit the timber of Northern Canada. He plans to use Indian labor. Sgt. Thorne is sent to investigate. His horse, Royal Red, and Silver Chief III help uphold the law.

O'Brien, John
5
Silver Chief's Revenge
Winston, 1954
  This was supposed to be the last book about Silver Chief and Thorne of the Mounted Police. The series ended with Mr. O'Brien's death. But another author wrote one more story.

Miller, Albert
6

Silver Chief's Big Game Trail
Holt, 1961
  Mr. Miller writes about Silver Chief after O'Brien's death. This book is about the brutal killing of animals across Canada and the Arctic Circle.

O'Dell, Scott
1
Island of the Blue Dolphins
Houghton, 1960
  The story of how a young girl, Karana, and her brother survived on a stranded island for 18 years. Her brother is killed by wild dogs and she must survive alone.

O'Dell, Scott
2
Zia
Houghton, 1976
  Zia is Karana's niece. Karana can't relate to people after her long isolation and prefers to be alone. Zia has problems of her own because of prejudices but Karana teaches her how to cope.

O'Dell, Scott
A1
Captive
Houghton, 1979
  As part of a Spanish expedition, Julian Escobar sees the enslavement of the Mayans. He is mistaken for the god Kukulcan, returning as predicted.

O'Dell, Scott
A2
Feathered Serpent
Houghton, 1981
  Julian sees the coming of Cortes and the capture of Tenochtitlan. He is still thought to be Kukulcan and travels to where the Aztecs live.

O'Dell, Scott
A3
Amethyst Ring
Houghton, 1983
  Julian witnesses the magnificence of the Incan Empire and its swift and tragic fall. Julian becomes a pearl trader for Pizarro who is robbing the Incas. He eventually returns to Spain in despair.

Ormondroyd, E.
1
Time at the Top
Parnassus, 1963

Susan rides up to the top floor of her building in an elevator and suddenly she is in another world. She is living in 1881. She moves back and forth and then takes her father with her.

Ormondroyd, E.
2
All in Good Time
Parnassus, 1975

Robert and Victoria Walker and their mother, and Susan and her father are involved in a series of adventures ending with Susan's father marrying Mrs. Walker.

Ottley, Reginald
1
Boy Alone
Harcourt, 1965

A young boy loves his dog Brolga but knows he must lose him to the Hunters. Brolga's puppy, Rags, and the boy become very attached and the boy does not want to give him up.

Ottley, Reginald
2
Roan Colt
Harcourt, 1966

A lame colt, destined to be shot, is hidden by the boy. He shows a great deal of courage in rescuing the colt from where he is penned, when a fire breaks out.

Ottley, Reginald
3
Rain Comes to Yamboorah
Harcourt, 1967

The story of a boy in Australia who works on a cattle station. He matures and accepts the plight of the people around him: the cook, the dogman and the two aborigine girls.

Palmer, Myron
1
Egyptian Necklace
Houghton, 1961

Tomb robbers and the rewards of capture is the theme of this story of ancient Egypt in 1400 B.C. Ar and his friend are the ones who help in the capture.

Palmer, Myron
2
Treachery in Crete
Houghton, 1961

The uncovering of a robbery plot puts Ar and his friends in great danger.

Parkinson, Ethelyn
1
Terrible Trouble of Rupert Piper
Abingdon, 1963

Rupert, Clayte, Dood and Milt make up the gang of boys that upset both school teachers and townspeople of Wakefield. They are not bad but can be annoyingly funny.

Parkinson, Ethelyn
2
Operation That Happened to Rupert Piper
Abingdon, 1966

Rupert substitutes for his friend Milt at the hospital so that Milt could be in a show. He has his appendix removed. He and his friends upset the entire hospital with their antics.

Parkinson, Ethelyn
3
Rupert Piper and Megan the Valuable Girl
Abingdon, 1972

Rupert and the boys must include a new girl in their activities. The town is trying to win the title of most typical American town. Everyone is acting "typical" and Megan is part of this act.

Parkinson, Ethelyn
4
Rupert Piper and the Dear, Dear Birds
Abingdon, 1976

Rupert and his friends lose their circus tickets in an encounter with a birdwatcher. They are so mad they form a Bird Haters Club and put out negative, false information about birds.

Parkinson, Ethelyn
5

**Rupert Piper
and the Boy Who Could Knit**
Abingdon, 1979

Shirley was a boy who knits and cooks. And admits liking girls! Rupert, Clayte, Dood, Hugh and Milt don't understand this. The girls meet Jamie who is a tomboy. Wakefield is not the same.

**Parkinson, Ethelyn
A1**
Good Old Archibald
Abingdon, 1960

Trent, Wilmer, and Harley can't keep up with Arch, a new arrival who will play baseball. But they had to turn Arch into a regular American boy.

**Parkinson, Ethelyn
A2**
Merry Mad Bachelors
Abingdon, 1962

Trent, Harley, Wilmer and Archibald wanted to be tall and make the basketball team. With the help of Emory, who is tall they hope to have a good team. But Emory can't live with his bachelor uncle.

**Peck, Richard
1**
Ghost Belonged to Me
Viking, 1975

Alex meets a curious female ghost. This begins a series of errie adventures. The ghost is predicting a tragedy. Alex and Blossom Culp must help.

**Peck, Richard
2**
Ghosts I Have Been
Viking, 1977

Comedy and tragedy beset Blossom Culp, the girl who has the gift of second-sight and can see the future. She lives in the early 1900s but can see into 1980.

**Peck, Richard
3**
Dreadful Future of Blossom Culp
Delacorte, 1983

Blossom Culp, a 14-year-old psychic, has comical, spooky adventures when she is hurtled into the future.

**Peck, Richard
4**
Blossom Culp and the Sleep of Death
Delacorte, 1986

Blossom Culp has second-sight and can see into the past. She and Alexander become involved with an Egyptian princess who needs help in restoring her stolen treasures.

**Peck, Robert
1**
Soup
Knopf, 1974

The fun and problems of two boys, Soup and Rob, growing up in a small town in Vermont. They and their friends keep the town in a frenzy most of the time.

**Peck, Robert
2**
Soup and Me
Knopf, 1975

Soup and his friends and all their trouble-making, innocent though it may be, is not always appreciated by others.

**Peck, Robert
3**
Soup for President
Knopf, 1978

Rob manages Soup's campaign for class president. Rob's girlfriend is also running. What will he do?

**Peck, Robert
4**
Soup's Drum
Knopf, 1980

Soup and Rob play the drum in the Fourth of July parade. Rob swears revenge when he realizes that he has carried the big drum for most of the parade. No wonder it was so heavy!

**Peck, Robert
5**
Soup on Wheels
Knopf, 1981

Soup and Rob try really hard to win a prize in their town's "Vermont Mardy Grah." They are sure their Zebra will win.

Peck, Robert
6
Soup in the Saddle
Knopf, 1983
Celebrating a special day for their teacher, Miss Kelly, Soup and Rob really do more good than harm to make the day successful.

Peck, Robert
7
Soup's Goat
Knopf, 1984
Cousin Sexton lends his unusual talent to Soup and Rob as they enter the town's goat-cart race.

Peck, Robert
8
Soup on Ice
Knopf, 1985
Rob and Soup engineer an incredible appearance by Santa and his sleigh in their small Vermont town.

Peck, Robert
9
Soup on Fire
Delacorte, 1987
Soup and Rob will do anything to get the attention of the visiting talent scout and their hero Fearless Ferguson.

Peck, Robert
10
Soup's Uncle
Delacorte, 1988
Vi, Soup's uncle, is a member of a motorcycle gang. At the last minute he is unable to ride in the important race. So Soup rides in his place!

Peck, Robert
A1
Trig
Little, 1977
A tomboy, Trig, gets a G-man machine gun as a present and "shoots" Aunt Augusta. Her two friends Skip and Bud suffer a bit from the consequences.

Peck, Robert
A2
Trig Sees Red
Little, 1978
Trig takes matters into her own hands when Clodsburg's only uniformed policeman is replaced by a traffic light.

Peck, Robert
A3
Trig Goes Ape
Little, 1980
Trig gets into an uproarious melee when Buck Fargo's wild Ape and Monkey show comes to town. Evelyn the mule and the scattered chickens add to the hilarity.

Peck, Robert
A4
Trig or Treat
Little, 1982
Trig masquerades as the seductive Delilah for the church Halloween costume pageant. Skip and Bud play Samson and Gideon.

Pellowski, Anne
1
First Farm in the Valley: Anna's Story
Philomel, 1982
Anna is a first. First to be born in America, first to own a farm in Wisconsin. But she dreams of returning to Poland.

Pellowski, Anne
2
Winding Valley Farm: Annie's Story
Philomel, 1982
Annie loved the farm and didn't want to move to the city. When the accident occurred she knew that she would not be leaving the farm.

Pellowski, Anne
3
Stairstep Farm: Anna Rose's Story
Philomel, 1981
Anna Rose is part of the third generation to grow up on the farm. She enjoys the work with her sisters and brothers but she wants to go to school.

Pellowski, Anne
4
Willow Wind Farm: Betsy's Story
Philomel, 1981
Betsy is the granddaughter of Annie.

She is one of ten children and is surrounded by family and extended family.

Pellowski, Anne
[

Betsy's Up-and-Down Year
Philomel, 1983
This is Betsy's story about life on the farm. She experiences jealousy among her brothers and sisters and sadness as older members of the family die.

Perl, Lila
1
Me and Fat Glenda
Houghton, 1972
Sara and her family move to a conservative town in New York from California where they lived nonconventionally. Sara makes friends with Glenda and helps her lose weight.

Perl, Lila
2
Hey, Remember Fat Glenda?
Houghton, 1981
This is Glenda's story of her battle against FAT. She does lose weight but it does not solve all of her problems such as a crush on her English teacher, her mother's eating plans, etc.

Perl, Lila
3
Fat Glenda's Summer Romance
Clarion, 1986
Glenda's weight problem returns after both friendship and romance turn out badly when the summer looked so promising. Her friends, Sara and Justin, seem to be distant and cool.

Petersen, P. J.
1
Would You Settle for Improbable
Delacorte, 1982
Mike and other ninth graders are influenced by Arnold, who spent time at a juvenile detention center. He helps Warren but when he wants to take Jennifer to the dance trouble sets in.

Petersen, P. J.
2

Here's to the Sophomores
Delacorte, 1984
Warren Cavendish becomes the best known and most controversial sophomore on campus, in just his first two weeks in high school.

Peyton, Karen
Pr1
Team
Crowell, 1975
Jonathan and Ruth, now 14, spend time with their horses as they plan their training and expectations. Both Ruth and Jonathan appear in other series.

Peyton, Karen
1
Prove Yourself a Hero
Collins, 1977
A kidnapping, a ransom, and a suspenseful search are the ingredients that make this story exciting. Jonathan questions his own character and must "prove himself a hero."

Peyton, Karen
2
Midsummer Night's Death
Collins, 1978
Jonathan's teacher is dead, and it is not suicide. So Jonathan begins his own investigation. He might be the next victim.

Peyton, Karen
3
Free Rein
Philomel, 1983
Jonathan, with too many problems at home, runs off with a friend to train a horse for the Grand National.

Peyton, Karen
A1
Flambards
World, 1967
Christina, an orphan, goes to live with her Uncle Russell at Flambards. She gets to know both her cousins, Mark and Will, and although she likes Will better she is destined to marry Mark.

Peyton, Karen
A2

Edge of a Cloud
World, 1968

Christina's love for William is shrouded by his devotion to flying. She marries him instead of Mark which upsets her Uncle Russell.

Peyton, Karen
A3
Flambards in Summer
World, 1969

The Russell's suffer generational conflicts within the family and also the tragedies of World War II. William is killed and Christina returns to Flambards.

Peyton, Karen
B1
Pennington's Last Term
Crowell, 1970

Pat Pennington tries to grow up in today's hectic society. Because of his nonconformist past and the trouble he has with any authority he almost loses the chance he wants most: a piano contest.

Peyton, Karen
B2
Beethoven's Medal
Crowell, 1971

Patrick is wild while his friend Ruth is quiet. He is both a serious music student and a young hoodlum. But he really likes Ruth. Ruth is also featured as a young girl in another series.

Peyton, Karen
B3
Pennington's Heir
Crowell, 1973

Pat and Ruth marry because of Ruth's pregnancy. This hampers Pat's musical career and is frowned upon by his family and friends.

Peyton, Karen
B4
Marion's Angels
Oxford Univ., 1979

Marion needs to raise money to save St. Michael's. Pat plays the piano to raise money for a church restoration. This is a "miracle" but another is needed to save Pat and Ruth's marriage.

Peyton, Karen
C1
Fly by Night
Oxford Univ., 1968

Twelve-year-old Ruth gets a pony, Fly, when she moves to the country. She worries about losing him when the family finances get strained. This is the same Ruth who appears in another series.

Peyton, Karen
C2
Team
Crowell, 1975

Ruth outgrows Fly and buys Toadhill Flax. Peter tells her it's too much horse for her. She needs to prove she is worthy of the horse and to belong to the Pony Club.

Philbrook, Clem
1
Ollie's Team
and the Baseball Computer
Hastings, 1967

A story full of practical jokes and mischief. Ollie's bulldog misbehaves, the boy next door, who is a pest, is thwarted and the baseball team competition increases with data from the computer.

Philbrook, Clem
2
Ollie's Team
and the Football Computer
Hastings, 1968

The computer both helps and hurts Ollie personally and his football team.

Philbrook, Clem
3
Ollie's Team
and the Basketball Computer
Hastings, 1969

Even though they have had trouble with computers and computer games in the past, Ollie is at it again. Their basketball team is as bad as their baseball and football team. They need help.

Philbrook, Clem
4
Ollie's Team Plays Biddy Baseball
Hastings, 1970

Ollie forgets that he must concentrate in order to win baseball games. He decides he is a drone after learning about bees in his science class and thereby loses a game for his team and more.

Philbrook, Clem
5
Ollie, the Backward Forward
Hastings, 1971
Does Winnie, the bulldog, really kill chickens? Bruce has a picture of him doing it. He tries to blackmail Ollie with it. Ollie refuses and Winnie is saved by a classroom trial.

Philbrook, Clem
6
Ollie's Team and the Alley Cats
Hastings, 1971
The Alley Cats are a girls' basketball team. They want to play the Bulldogs, a boys' team. The girls win but the boys ask for a rematch with five players on each team (girls have six) and win.

Philbrook, Clem
7
Ollie's Team
and the 200-Pound Problem
Hastings, 1972
Jumbo has gained so much weight he can't field balls and can't hit balls. He was the team's best hitter. He is programmed into positive thinking: THINK THIN. He lost 25 pounds.

Philbrook, Clem
8
Ollie's Team
and the Million Dollar Mistake
Hastings, 1973
Ollie is tied up with bank robbers and a bank mistake. He is afraid of losing his spot on the baseball team. He keeps making excuses about his size but it's his thinking that's at fault.

Pierce, Meredith
1
Dark-Angle
Little, 1982
A servant girl, Aeriel, must decide whether to save or destroy her vampire master. Does his obvious greatness overpower his evil deeds?

Pierce, Meredith
?
Gathering of Gargoyles
Little, 1984
The White Witch has made gargoyles out of the mortals she has enslaved. Aeriel must free Irrylath from the White Witch's spell.

Pierce, Tamara
1
Alanna, First Adventure
Atheneum, 1983
The story of Alanna. A fantasy with medieval flavor, as Alanna, posing as a boy, becomes a page and then a squire to the Prince.

Pierce, Tamara
2
In the Hand of the Goddess
Atheneum, 1984
Alanna conceals the fact that she is a girl, and pursues knighthood. But, she fears sorcery is being used against her. She is Squire to Prince Jonathon, who knows she is a girl.

Pierce, Tamara
3
Woman Who Rides Like a Man
Atheneum, 1986
Alanna influences a desert tribe by changing the role of women. She teaches them to be Shamams, a role meant for men only. She also continues to mature and succeed in her field.

Pierce, Tamara
4
Lioness Rampant
Atheneum, 1988
Alanna travels to the Roof of the World to get the Dominon Jewels. She meets many challenges, both dangerous and surprising.

Pinkwater, Daniel
1
Snarkout Boys
and the Avocado of Death
Lothrop, 1982

Walter, Winston and Rat have an adventure involving a mad scientist and the Chicken Man.

Pinkwater, Daniel
2
*Snarkout Boys
and the Baconburg Horror*
Lothrop, 1984
Walter, Winston and Rat have an adventure involving a beatnik poet and a werewolf.

Platt, Kin
1
Chloris and the Creeps
Chilton, 1973
Chloris' mother's boyfriend is the Creep. When she marries him Chloris causes trouble. She idolizes her dead father but she comes around to accept her new father.

Platt, Kin
2
Chloris and the Freaks
Bradbury, 1975
Jenny is hooked on astrological signs. Her sister Chloris thinks Jenny is a Freak. Chloris feels her dead father wants her mother to divorce Fidel, her new husband.

Platt, Kin
3
Chloris and the Weirdos
Bradbury, 1978
Chloris tells about life with her mother and sister, as she sees it. Jenny's boyfriends are the weirdos, as are her own. Chloris and her mother have a bitter argument and she leaves.

Platt, Kin
A1
Sinbad and Me
Delacorte, 1966
A funny and frightening mystery cleverly solved by Sinbad, the dog, and Steve.

Platt, Kin
A2
Mystery of the Witch Who Wouldn't
Chilton, 1969

Steve and his dog, Sinbad, solve the criminal activities of the Satanists. The crime was predicted by a witch.

Platt, Kin
A3
Ghost of Hellshire Street
Delacorte, 1980
Steve, Sinbad and their friends get involved with a kidnapped scientist, a weird psychic, Sheriff Landry and a pirate ghost.

Plowman, Stephanie
1
Three Lives for the Czar
Houghton, 1969
Andrei lives with his family in Russia during the reign of Nicholas II. The story implies that the Revolution may not have happened if Nicholas was a kinder man.

Plowman, Stephanie
2
My Kingdom for a Grave
Houghton, 1971
Andrei relates life up to World War I. He tells about the Czar and Rasputin. He tries to help his family escape but fails. He later learns of their death and burial.

Pope, Ray
1
Strosa Light
Hart Davis, 1965
Frank and his brother Dave help Strosa Lighthouse keepers when a trawler runs aground.

Pope, Ray
2
Salvage from Strosa
Hart Davis, 1967
Frank and Dave give aid to an escaping seaman and claim a trawler as salvage.

Potter, Mariam
1
Blatherskite
Morrow, 1980
Life on a farm during the Great Depression is hard but also has its

moments of merriment for a ten-year-old.

Potter, Mariam
?
Chance Wild Apple
Morrow, 1982
What adventure does a discovered tree bring?

Prince, Alison
1
Sinister Airfield
Morrow, 1983
Finding a body in an abandoned airfield causes three teens to wonder about rustlers. Jan, Harrie and Neil help to capture the thieves.

Prince, Alison
2
Night Landings
Morrow, 1984
Jan, Harrie and Neil are sure that smugglers are operating in the nearby airfield.

Reiss, Johanna
1
Upstairs Room
Crowell, 1972
A Jewish family, although separated, survived the German persecution. They stayed in farmers' homes for three years when the Nazis occupied Holland. Now Annie and Simi must face the future.

Reiss, Johanna
2
Journey Back
Crowell, 1976
After spending three years in hiding this Jewish family is reunited. Annie, Simi and Rachel begin to rebuild their lives. Their father remarries.

Richter, Conrad
1
Light in the Forest
Knopf, 1966
Story of a teenaged boy's dilemma in deciding where he wants to grow up—in an Indian culture or that of the White man.

Richter, Conrad
2
Country of Strangers
Knopf, 1966
This is the story of a White girl captured by the Indians who must return to her original parents.

Rinaldi, Ann
1
But in the Fall I'm Leaving
Holiday, 1985
Brie plans to leave her too-strict father and live with the mother who abandoned her as a baby. But she learns that Miss Emily, whose house she spray-painted, is her maternal grandmother.

Rinaldi, Ann
2
Good Side of My Heart
Holiday, 1987
Brie is 16 and has a friend, Josh, who is a senior. She has a brother and a strict father who doesn't like Josh. She finds out that Josh is a homosexual and is confused.

Rinaldi, Ann
A1
Term Paper
Walker, 1980
Nicki's brother assigns her a topic for a term paper: death in the family. Her brother resents his responsibility for her.

Rinaldi, Ann
A2
Promises Are for Keeping
Holiday, 1982
Nicki is 15 and an orphan. She is caught stealing birth control pills from her brother's desk. This only adds to the trouble she already has with him.

Roberts, Willo
1
Minder Curse
Atheneum, 1978
Danny, his grandfather and Leroy, the dog, are always at the scene of minor disasters. But a prize canine, a pedigree Silky Terrier has been stolen. Danny, C.B. and Paul solve the case.

Roberts, Willo
2
More Minder Curses
Atheneum, 1980
   Danny helps the Caspitorian sisters (the cat ladies) when they think their house is haunted because they have seen faces in the window. Danny wants to capture Killer Cat while he's there.

Robertson, Keith
1
Henry Reed, Inc.
Viking, 1958
   Henry Reed, who has been away from America most of his life, comes back for the summer and starts a business: "HENRY REED, RESEARCH." He and Midge do turtle painting and truffle hunting.

Robertson, Keith
2
Henry Reed's Journey
Viking, 1963
   Henry, his friend Midge and her family travel from San Francisco to New Jersey, where he will spend the summer. He keeps a journal of Hopi Indian parade, horned toads, etc.

Robertson, Keith
3
Henry Reed's Baby Sitting Service
Viking, 1966
   In New Jersey, Henry and Midge continue to run their research service.

Robertson, Keith
4
Henry Reed's Big Show
Viking, 1970
   Henry's going to become a great theatrical producer. He starts in Graver's Corner and before the summer is over, he had put on a rock music festival and a wild western rodeo.

Robertson, Keith
5
Henry Reed's Think Tank
Viking, 1986
   Henry and Midge are now consultants for Grover Corner. They can barely solve the problems they are asked to handle: Rodney's weight problem, Deirdre's allowance, Willy and Betsy's food, etc.

Robertson, Keith
A1
Three Stuffed Owls
Viking, 1954
   The Carson Street Detective Agency made up of Neil and Swede look for a lost bicycle. Instead they find diamond smugglers and Three Stuffed Owls.

Robertson, Keith
A2
Money Machine
Viking, 1969
   Neil and Swede look for counterfeiters. They are trapped in the cellar and do, by accident, discover the printing press.

Rodgers, Mary
1
Freaky Friday
Harper, 1972
   A mother and daughter find themselves in each other's shoes. They both find this surprising, enlightening and disastrous.

Rodgers, Mary
2
Billion for Boris
Harper, 1974
   Annabel and her friends encounter adventures which don't work out as planned. Ape-face (Ben) fixes Boris' television and they find that they can see into the near future.

Rodgers, Mary
3
Summer Switch
Harper, 1982
   This time father and son find themselves in each others shoes and have the same surprising and enlightening experiences. Father goes to summer camp and Ben flies to L.A. on business.

Sachs, Marilyn
1
Veronica Ganz
Doubleday, 1968

Veronica, who is big for her age, bullies everyone at school. She made Laura's school life difficult and now Peter, a new boy at school, is the target of her plots.

Sachs, Marilyn

2

Peter and Veronica

Doubleday, 1969

Veronica and Peter have become friends but Peter realizes this causes problems. Prejudice on the part of both mothers puts pressure on their friendship. Veronica is Gentile, Peter is Jewish.

Sachs, Marilyn

3

Marv

Doubleday, 1970

The story is about invincible Marv, who no one really understands. He is a classmate of Veronica and Peter. He tries hard to compete with his older sister who is very bright.

Sachs, Marilyn

4

Truth about Mary Rose

Doubleday, 1973

Mary Rose, Veronica's daughter, investigates the truth about her late aunt, Mary Rose, who is her namesake. Was she the heroine who saved tenants in an apartment fire, or not?

Sachs, Marilyn

A1

Amy Moves In

Doubleday, 1964

Amy and her sister Laura have all the problems of any youngster who has moved to a new neighborhood: making friends, finding out where everything is and enrolling in a new school.

Sachs, Marilyn

A2

Laura's Luck

Doubleday, 1965

Laura and Amy go to camp and Amy makes friends right away while Laura is hanging back. But, in time, she learns to love camp.

Sachs, Marilyn

A3

Amy and Laura

Doubleday, 1966

Amy and Laura's mother returns from the hospital but she has changed a great deal in the year she was away and Laura must adjust. She also meets Veronica who appears in another series.

Sachs, Marilyn

B1

Bear's House

Doubleday, 1971

Fran doesn't fit in with her classmates. Her homelife is hopeless. If she works very hard at school and gets good grades she could win the Bear's House which she dearly loves.

Sachs, Marilyn

B2

Fran Ellen's House

Dutton, 1987

After being placed in a foster home Fran and her brother are together. The Bear's House now has a different role to play in Fran's life.

Sebestyen, Ouida

1

Words by Heart

Little, 1979

A young Black girl, Lena, struggles to fulfill her papa's dreams of a better future for their family, in spite of prejudices. She saves Tater, even though he's the one that killed her papa.

Sebestyen, Ouida

2

On Fire

Little, 1985

The adventures of two brothers during a dangerous strike in 1911. Tater's life is spared but he has to live with the thought that he killed Lena's father. His brother Sammy helps him cope.

Selden, George

1

Cricket in Times Square

Farrar, 1960

Chester Cricket lives in the Times Square subway. He shares it with Harry

Cat and Tucker Mouse. He plays classical music and goes to concerts. His music makes the Bellini family famous.

Selden, George
2
Tucker's Countryside
Farrar, 1969
The further adventures of Chester Cricket. Harry Cat and Tucker Mouse come to Connecticut for a visit and help Chester with his problem of expanding housing.

Selden, George
3
Harry Cat's Pet Puppy
Farrar, 1974
Harry brings her new friend, a puppy, to live in the subway with Tucker but he soon grows too big for that home and must find a new one.

Selden, George
4
Chester Cricket's Pigeon Ride
Farrar, 1981
Lulu Pigeon takes Chester for a ride he will never forget. He views the Manhattan skyline at night. A slight story.

Selden, George
5
Chester Cricket's New Home
Farrar, 1983
Cricket's home collapses and he must find a new one but has has problems that his friends try to help solve even though he is so picky and the chore gets tedious.

Senn, Steve
1
Spacebread
Atheneum, 1981
A large, white wondercat moves among the stars looking for a stolen buckle and to avenge a murder. Sonto, her friend, is killed in battle.

Senn, Steve
2
Born of Flame

Atheneum, 1982
Spacebread meets Niral, who is running away and helps him. Quon wounds Klimmit and Spacebread must find a way to cure him.

Sharmat, Marjorie
1
How to Meet a Gorgeous Guy
Delacorte, 1983
Shari and Lisa are high school students. Shari gets her date with Craig and Lisa writes an article for the school paper. But neither challenge comes without problems.

Sharmat, Marjorie
2
How to Meet a Gorgeous Girl
Delacorte, 1984
Mark tries to interest Meg in romance by tips he learned from a book called "How to Meet a Gorgeous Girl."

Sharmat, Marjorie
A1
Getting Something
on Maggie Marmelstein
Harper, 1971
Thad tells everyone that Maggie squeaks like a mouse. Maggie tells everyone about Thad's cooking. And so it goes.

Sharmat, Marjorie
A2
Maggie Marmelstein for President
Harper, 1975
Maggie decides to help Thad run for school office. But runs against him herself when he doesn't ask her to become his campaign manager.

Sharmat, Marjorie
A3
Mysteriously Yours,
Maggie Marmelstein
Harper, 1982
Maggie writes a mystery column in the school newspaper. In this capacity she learns that responsibility goes with power.

Sharmat, Marjorie
B1

He Noticed I'm Alive
Delacorte, 1985
  Jody and Matt are having problems because Matt's mother and Jody's father are dating.

Sharmat, Marjorie
B2
Two Guys Noticed Me
Delacorte, 1985
  Jody's father is now engaged to Matt's mother and the troubles continue. Jody meets Travis, a fellow art student and he shows some attention but Jody still likes Matt.

Sharp, Margery
1
Rescuers
Little, 1959
  A poet is rescued from the Black Castle by Miss Bianca, Nils and their friends, when Bernard asks for the help of the Prisoner's Aid Society.

Sharp, Margery
2
Miss Bianca
Little, 1962
  The Mouse Prisoner's Aid Society, with Miss Bianca and Bernard, rescue Patience from a palace where she is held by an evil Duchess.

Sharp, Margery
3
Turret
Little, 1963
  The evil Mandrake is prisoner in the turret. A rescue is planned for midnight, even though he is Miss Bianca's enemy.

Sharp, Margery
4
Miss Bianca in the Salt Mines
Little, 1966
  Miss Bianca and Bernard attempt to rescue Teddy from his cruel jailer in the salt mines.

Sharp, Margery
5
Miss Bianca in the Orient
Little, 1970
  Miss Bianca and Bernard on their most dangerous mission. They must save a court page from death at the hands of Ranee.

Sharp, Margery
6
Miss Bianca in the Antarctic
Heinemann, 1970
  Miss Bianca and Bernard need all the strength they can muster to survive when they are left in the Antarctic.

Sharp, Margery
7
Miss Bianca and the Bridesmaid
Little, 1972
  When the ambassador's daughter's bridesmaid disappears before the wedding Miss Bianca must solve the mystery.

Sharp, Margery
8
Bernard the Brave
Little, 1977
  Miss Bianca is away and Bernard has an adventure on his own. He rescues an orphan heiress who has been kidnapped.

Sharp, Margery
9
Bernard into Battle
Little, 1978
  Miss Bianca's faithful Bernard repulses an army of rats that live in the Ambassador's cellar.

Singer, Marilyn
1
Case of the Sabotaged School Play
Harper, 1984
  A boring school play becomes big news when stage sabotage is suspected. A good case for Sam and Dave to solve.

Singer, Marilyn
2
Leroy Is Missing
Harper, 1984
  Sam and Dave help Rita look for her missing eight-year-old brother. They follow false clues and run into danger. Leroy does turn up with an unsuspected explanation.

Singer, Marilyn
3
Case of the Cackling Car
Harper, 1985

Sam and Dave interrupt their Texas vacation to search for a missing girl. Someone is smuggling pet birds into the country.

Singer, Marilyn
4
Clue in Code
Harper, 1985

Money for the class trip suddenly disappears. Did the class bully, Willie, the custodian's son who has stolen before, take it? Sam and Dave have a mystery to solve.

Singer, Marilyn
5
Case of the Fixed Election
Harper, 1989

Dave runs for student council president. He is accused of stuffing the ballot box. Sam must clear Dave's name.

Singer, Marilyn
6
Hoax Is on You
Harper, 1989

Sam and Dave enter a magazine contest for the best hoax. A foreign exchange student, Dardanella, is really not an exchange student, not a thief, but a hoax.

Singer, Marilyn
A1
Fido Frame-Up
Warne, 1983

Sam Spayed, is a dog sidekick for Philip. A cameo is stolen. Sam gets information from other dogs and the theft is solved.

Singer, Marilyn
A2
Nose for Trouble
Holt, 1985

Philip and Sam have been hired by a cosmetic company to find out who is leaking secrets. Sam again solves the mystery.

Singer, Marilyn
B1
Tarantulas on the Brain
Harper, 1982

Lizzie is interested in science. She tries to earn money to buy a tarantula, but dishonesty and misunderstanding mars her attempt.

Singer, Marilyn
B2
Lizzie Silver of Sherwood Forest
Harper, 1986

Lizzie is interested in Robin Hood. She and Tessa go to the fair where she meets Andy who teaches her how to be a one-man band. She wants to go to music school with Tessa.

Skolsky, Mindy
1
Whistling Teakettle
Harper, 1977

This is a picture of New York City during the Great Depression.

Skolsky, Mindy
2
Carnival and Kopeck
Harper, 1979

Problems arise between Hannah and her grandmother. Hannah learns that closeness always has some problems.

Skolsky, Mindy
3
Hannah Is a Palindrome
Harper, 1980

Hannah's family moves into an apartment at the rear of a restaurant. She sees herself and her family in a different light.

Skolsky, Mindy
4
*Hannah and the Best
Father on Route 9W*
Harper, 1982

. Hannah and her father compete in separate contests. But they are also supportive of each other.

Sleigh, B.
1
Carbonel, King of the Cats

Bobbs Merrill, 1955

Carbonel, an extraordinary black cat, is under a witch's spell. Rosemary and her friend, John, must break the spell.

Sleigh, B.
2
Kingdom of Carbonel
Bobbs Merrill, 1960

Rosemary and John take care of Carbonel's kitten while he is away fighting for his kingdom. They both can understand what animals say because of a secret potion they got from a witch.

Slepian, Janice
1
Alfred Summer
Macmillan, 1980

Four youngsters and a boat have a courageous, quixotic quest that nearly ends in tragedy. All the children are handicapped in some way and form a tight circle of friendship.

Slepian, Janice
2
Lester's Turn
Macmillan, 1981

A story of disabled youngsters and how they cope with their problems. Lester tries to help Alfred because he feels he is deteriorating in the hospital, but his plan doesn't work out.

Slote, Alfred
1
My Robot Buddy
Lippincott, 1975

Jack lives in the future where robots look and act like people. Jack has a robot he calls Danny One. A robotnapper tries to steal him.

Slote, Alfred
2
My Trip to Alpha I
Lippincott, 1978

VOYA-CODE, a means of travel for Jack and Danny One, takes them where his aunt is in a dummy body.

Slote, Alfred
3
C.O.L.A.R.

Lippincott, 1981

C.O.L.A.R. is a planet inhabited by the robots Dr. Atkins invented. Jack and his family are stranded on this planet.

Slote, Alfred
4
Omega Station
Lippincott, 1983

Jack and his robot, Danny One, must save the universe from a mad scientist, Otto Drago.

Slote, Alfred
5
Trouble on Janus
Lippincott, 1985

Jack and his robot, Danny One, go to Janus to rescue King Paul, a 12-year-old ruler. There is a robot look-alike to complicate the rescue.

Slote, Alfred
A1
Moving Inn
Lippincott, 1988

Robbie and Peggy try to keep their father from marrying the person he's considering. They try to fix him up with a person of their liking, Carol.

Slote, Alfred
A2
Friends Like That
Lippincott, 1988

Robbie is upset when Carol, the person he wants his father to marry, gets married. He has further problems because he might lose his shortstop position on the team. So he runs away.

Smaridge, Norah
1
Secret of the Brownstone House
Dodd, 1977

Robin is vacationing in New York and discovers two runaways hiding in an old brownstone house where two boys were murdered years ago. Elly is returned to her home and Len, an orphan, is befriended.

Smaridge, Norah
2
Mystery at Greystone Hall

Dodd, 1979

Robin goes to England and meets Mark and Miss Tilly. They tour Greystone Hall and are invited to stay for a week. But they didn't anticipate being grabbed by a statue or being locked in a cellar.

Smaridge, Norah
3
Mystery in the Old Mansions
Dodd, 1981

Robin is a summer guide where her aunt works in a mansion similar to the one where she lives. A formula for making a pottery glaze is missing. Robin solves this and finds a missing teen, also.

Smaridge, Norah
4
Mysteries in the Commune
Dodd, 1982

Robin befriends Emmy, who thinks her mother is not her real one, and Adam who is running away. She and her friend Jerry try to straighten this out.

Smith, Dodie
1
Hundred and One Dalmations
Viking, 1957

Someone is kidnapping the Dalmations. The mystery is solved by the parents of a kidnapped litter: Pongo and Missis.

Smith, Dodie
2
Starlight Barking
Viking, 1968

The dog world is faced with a time and space problem. Time is suspended for all human beings. All animals except dogs are asleep. The Dalmations assume control.

Smith, Doris
1
Last Was Lloyd
Viking, 1981

Lloyd, fat and overprotected, is teased because he is not chosen for the school team but soon everyone sees a different Lloyd. Ancil, his friend, is his model of confidence and independence.

Smith, Doris
2
First Hard Times
Viking, 1983

Ancil doesn't like her new stepfather because she is still loyal to her father who was reported missing in Vietnam ten years ago.

Snyder, Zilpha
1
Below the Root
Atheneum, 1975

Raamo questions the teachings of the land of Green-Sky and uncovers deceptions about the tree. The enemy is Poshshan who lives under the roots and steals babies.

Snyder, Zilpha
2
And All Between
Atheneum, 1976

Raamo and his friends are in great danger because of secrets and discoveries. Kindar and the Endlings use their separate powers to get reunited.

Snyder, Zilpha
3
Until the Celebration
Atheneum, 1977

Mounting tension is soothed by two children who have become symbols of unification between the Endlings and the Kindar.

Snyder, Zilpha
A1
Headless Cupid
Atheneum, 1971

Amanda's family moves into a house that is haunted when her mother remarries. Amanda believes in the supernatural and uses this to justify her aloofness toward David and her new family. But . . .

Snyder, Zilpha
A2
Famous Stanley Kidnapping Case
Atheneum, 1979

A gang of kidnappers run off with Amanda and the four Stanley children in Italy because of Amanda's boasting of her father's wealth.

Snyder, Zilpha
A3
Blair's Nightmare
Atheneum, 1984

Blair really does see a dog at night but no one believes him. Finally the rest of the children see the dog, too, and complications begin. Can they keep the dog? Will David improve in school?

Sobol, Donald
1
Encyclopedia Brown, Boy Detective
Lodestar, 1963

Match wits with Encyclopedia Brown as he solves his many mysteries. He listens, observes and trains his memory.

Sobol, Donald
2
Encyclopedia Brown
and the Case of the Secret Pitch
Lodestar, 1978

Bugs has a deal with Speedy about his baseball bat but. . . . Ten more mysteries with Encyclopedia Brown.

Sobol, Donald
3
Encyclopedia Brown Finds the Clues
Lodestar, 1966

Try your wits again with Encyclopedia Brown as he tackles more astounding puzzles.

Sobol, Donald
4
Encyclopedia Brown Gets His Man
Lodestar, 1967

These puzzlers have stumped elders but Encyclopedia Brown solves them.

Sobol, Donald
5
Encyclopedia Brown Solves Them All
Lodestar, 1977

Encyclopedia Brown, the clever detective, is back with more puzzles to solve.

Sobol, Donald
6
Encyclopedia Brown Keeps the Peace
Lodestar, 1973

How good a detective are you? Can you keep up with Encyclopedia Brown?

Sobol, Donald
7
Encyclopedia Brown Saves the Day
Lodestar, 1970

More adventures with Encyclopedia Brown and Sally as they solve more mysteries.

Sobol, Donald
8
Encyclopedia Brown
Tracks Them Down
Lodestar, 1971

Encyclopedia Brown, a super sleuth, solves more baffling mysteries.

Sobol, Donald
9
Encyclopedia Brown Shows the Way
Lodestar, 1972

The Brown Detective Agency has a girl to contend with in this case.

Sobol, Donald
10
Encyclopedia Brown Takes the Case
Lodestar, 1973

Ten all new Encyclopedia Brown mysteries.

Sobol, Donald
11
Encyclopedia Brown Lends a Hand
Lodestar, 1974

The solution to ten mysteries are solved by Leroy "Encyclopedia" Brown.

Sobol, Donald
12
Encyclopedia Brown
and the Case of the Dead Eagles
Lodestar, 1975

There are enough clues so that the reader can solve the case before Encyclopedia Brown.

Sobol, Donald
13
Encyclopedia Brown
and the Case of the Midnight Visitor
Lodestar, 1977

Bank robbers, kidnappers and Chicago gangsters—Encyclopedia Brown takes them all on and solves ten more new cases.

Sobol, Donald
14
Encyclopedia Brown Carries On
Four Winds, 1980
Encyclopedia Brown is a lucky sleuth with a father who is chief of police.

Sobol, Donald
15
Encyclopedia Brown Sets the Pace
Four Winds, 1982
A printing is stolen and Encyclopedia Brown must find the thief.

Sobol, Donald
16
Encyclopedia Brown and the Case of the Mysterious Handprints
Morrow, 1985
Encyclopedia Brown and Sally have ten more mysteries to solve. There is a case of missing property, one of sabotaged races and eight others.

Sobol, Donald
17
Encyclopedia Brown and the Case of the Exploding Plumbing
Scholastic, 1984
See if you can solve the mystery before the great Encyclopedia Brown does.

Sobol, Donald
18
Encyclopedia Brown and the Case of the Treasure Hunt
Morrow, 1988
How does a puzzle lead to a thief? Encyclopedia Brown and Sally will find out in these ten new mysteries.

Sommer-Bodenburg, Angela
1
My Friend the Vampire
Dial, 1984
While Tony watches a horror movie Rudolph, a kid vampire comes in. He and Tony become friends and Tony meets Rudolph's family and Tony's family meets him.

Sommer-Bodenburg, Angela
2
Vampire Moves In
Dial, 1984
Rudolph is banned from his family's vault and moves in with Tony. Tony tries to hide the coffin and the fact that he is there.

Sommer-Bodenburg, Angela
3
Vampire Takes a Trip
Dial, 1985
Tony is sure that his vacation is going to be a total bust. But his friend Rudolph, the vampire, will come along if they can find a way to transport him unseen and unknown by anyone.

Southall, Ivan
1
King of the Sticks
Greenwillow, 1979
Custard, because he is thought to be special, is kidnapped by the sons of the man Custard's mother asks to help find him.

Southall, Ivan
2
Golden Goose
Greenwillow, 1981
Slow-witted Custard is forced to search for gold. Even Preacher Tom, who set out to rescue him, believes he can find gold. Custard becomes known as the "Golden Goose."

Spearing, Judith
1
Ghost That Went to School
Atheneum, 1967
The Temple's lived in an old house; Mr. and Mrs. Temple, Wilbur and Mortimer. They were ghosts. Wilbur was bored and wanted to go to school. He caused a great deal of trouble but made some friends.

Spearing, Judith
2
Museum Ghosts
Atheneum, 1969
All four Temples helped the workmen as they remodeled the old house to be a museum. They tried to stay out of it but couldn't help picking up things and aiding with the heavy work.

Spinelli, Jerry
1
Space Station Seventh Grade
Little, 1982
Jason learns about communal show-ers, pimples, girls, sports and the awful ninth graders. A boy's "Are you there, God . . . ?"

Spinelli, Jerry
2
Jason and Marceline
Little, 1986
This continues the story of Jason in junior high school. He is a bit more adjusted to growing up. His knowledge of girls has improved and he is accepting adulthood.

Springstubb, Tricia
1
Which Way to the Nearest Wilderness
Little, 1984
Eunice, 11, and her best friend Joy start a personalized card service: When You Care Enough To Give The Very Worst. A poison pen type card. Eunice sickens of it and breaks away.

Springstubb, Tricia
2
Eunice Gottlieb
and the Unwhitewashed
Truth about Life
Delacorte, 1987
Eunice and Joy have a catering business: Have Your Cake. But Joy is falling for a boy from school. Eunice can't believe it and they argue. She takes Reggie as a partner but it is not working out.

Springstubb, Tricia
3
Eunice (The Egg Salad) Gottlieb
Little, 1988
Joy is a natural at gymnastics but Eunice isn't. She's afraid she will embarrass everyone, including herself. But because of Joy's friendship and encouragement she does very well.

Spykman, Elizabeth
1
Lemon and a Star
Harcourt, 1955

The story of the four Care's children who grew up in the early 1900s. They are motherless and free to do as they please because father is busy. Father remarries and they get a mother.

Spykman, Elizabeth
2
Wild Angel
Harcourt, 1957
The four children have difficulty adjusting to a new mother and restrictions. But Father is still the same and encourages their misadventures.

Spykman, Elizabeth
3
Terrible, Horrible Edie
Harcourt, 1960
This story is about the Care's family. It concentrates on ten-year-old Edie, the youngest, and her summers adventure.

Spykman, Elizabeth
4
Edie on the Warpath
Harcourt, 1966
Edie rebels because she is the middle sibling of the Care's family. No one wants to take care of Edie when her mother must go away. Left almost alone, she and Susan have troublesome fun.

Stevenson, Drew
1
Case of the Horrible Swamp Monster
Dodd, 1984
Verna and Raymond make a home film of the swamp monster and "find" him. With the help of J. Huntley English, Monster Hunter, they solve the mystery and catch some robbers with money in the swamp.

Stevenson, Drew
2
Case of the Visiting Vampire
Dodd, 1986
Verna and Raymond, with the ever-present J. Huntley English, look for vampires. They suspect the actor who has the lead in "The Count of Castle Dracula." He is a defector from behind the Iron Curtain.

Stolz, Mary
1
Ferris Wheel
Harper, 1977
   Polly and Kate have been best friends all their lives. But Kate's family is going to move to California and Polly is crushed, especially since Kate seems to be looking forward to it.

Stolz, Mary
2
Cider Days
Harper, 1978
   A young girl, Polly, is persistent in her overtures toward a shy, new neighbor that results in a friendship.

Stolz, Mary
A1
Go Catch a Flying Fish
Harper, 1979
   Taylor, a teenager, tries to make Jem and B.J. adjust to the fact of their parent's separation. She and her brother, Jem, cope with their mother's frustration and their father's reaction.

Stolz, Mary
A2
What Time of Night Is It?
Harper, 1981
   Taylor, Jem and B.J. attempt to rebuild their family after their mother has deserted them. Granny Reddick is called to help. Mother does return and perhaps all will be well.

Stolz, Mary
B1
Dog on Barkham Street
Harper, 1960
   Edward has two problems. One, he wants a dog. Uncle Josh and Argess, his dog, take care of that. Two, Martin, the bully who lives next door. That remains a problem.

Stolz, Mary
B2
Bully on Barkham Street
Harper, 1963
   This is the story of the Dog on Barkham Street told from the point of view of Martin. Maybe he isn't the bully and aggressive boy he appears to be.

Stolz, Mary
B3
Explorer of Barkham Street
Harper, 1985
   Martin, the bully, reforms after losing his dog and explores the neighborhood. He makes good friends with his fantasy tales.

Strasser, Todd
1
Rock 'n' Roll Nights
Delacorte, 1983
   Gary is the lead guitarist for a rock group with Susan, Karl and Oscar. This story tells of the work and effort necessary to make a successful rock band.

Strasser, Todd
2
Turn It Up
Delacorte, 1984
   Gary and his Rock 'n' Roll band try to make the "big time" but he is careless and hurts himself and his band.

Sutcliff, Rosemary
A1
Light Beyond the Forest
Dutton, 1980
   The first in a series about King Arthur and the search for the Grail.

Sutcliff, Rosemary
A2
Sword and the Circle
Dutton, 1981
   Retells the adventures of King Arthur, Sir Lancelot and the other knights of the Round Table.

Sutcliff, Rosemary
A3
Road to Camlann
Dutton, 1982
   The evil Mordred, plotting against his father, King Arthur, implicates the Queen and Sir Lancelot in treachery.

Symons, Geraldine
1
Work House Child
Macmillan, 1969
   Pansy and Atalanta are under the supervision of absent-minded Nonna;

Pansy changes clothes with Leah from the workhouse. She is mistaken for a workhouse slave and reform changes are the outcome.

Symons, Geraldine
2
Miss Rivers and Miss Bridges
Macmillan, 1971

Pansy and Atalanta, disguised as Miss Rivers and Miss Bridges, take part in the campaign of the suffragettes in London. They land in jail and also in the newspapers.

Sypher, Lucy
1
Edge of Nowhere
Atheneum, 1972

Lucy makes three wishes on New Year's Eve, 1916. 1. Something grown up happens to her. 2. A dog. 3. A girl her age moves to town. All three wishes come true.

Sypher, Lucy
2
Cousins and Circuses
Atheneum, 1974

Lucy lives in Wales, North Dakota and likes it. Gwin moves to town with her minister father and sees everything as evil. Lucy sees fairs and girls' clubs, not scandal and corruption.

Sypher, Lucy
3
Spell of the Northern Lights
Atheneum, 1975

Lucy is afraid of many things, some real and some imagined. Some of her fears come to pass such as losing her dog. But some good things happen like her mother having a baby.

Sypher, Lucy
4
Turnabout Year
Atheneum, 1976

Lucy wants to go to high school in the city but it is just prior to World War I and her mother has a new baby. It looks like city school is out of the question.

Tannen, Mary
1

Wizard Children of Finn
Knopf, 1981

Bran and Fiona move into the past because of a Druid spell. They have historic adventures in ancient Ireland.

Tannen, Mary
2
Lost Legend of Finn
Knopf, 1982

Bran and Fiona have access to a magic book which helps transport them back to ancient Ireland. They found Uncle Rupert in A.D. 839.

Tapp, K.
1
Moth-Kin Magic
Atheneum, 1983

Ripple is less than one-inch tall. She, her mother and uncle are trapped by the giants in a glass jar used to study plant life. They must find a way to escape.

Tapp, K.
2
Flight of the Moth-Kin
Atheneum, 1987

Ripple and her family are released from the glass jar and are living in a forest where they encounter large insects and other dangers as they find their way back home to the river.

Taylor, Mildred
1
Song of the Trees
Dial, 1975

In this book Cassie is only eight years old and witnesses White men chopping down trees on her father's land. We meet Cassie later in the outstanding "Roll of Thunder . . . ."

Taylor, Mildren
2
Roll of Thunder, Hear My Cry
Dial, 1976

A moving story of survival of Cassie and her Black family in the South during the Great Depression. Her proud family owns land and struggles to keep up the taxes.

Taylor, Mildred
3

Let the Circle Be Unbroken
Dial, 1981

Four Black children experience racism and hard times but learn from their parents the pride and self-respect they need to survive.

Taylor, Sydney
1
All-of-a-Kind Family
Follett, 1951

Five little Jewish girls grow up in New York's Lower East Side before World War I. Sara is featured in this book.

Taylor, Sydney
2
More All-of-a-Kind Family
Follett, 1954

The girls spend their last year in the old neighborhood enjoying the Old World customs of 1914. And they have a new baby brother, Charles.

Taylor, Sydney
3
All-of-a-Kind Family Downtown
Follett, 1972

In this book the five sisters and Charlie are involved with their newly orphaned neighbor, Guido.

Taylor, Sydney
4
All-of-a-Kind Family Uptown
Follett, 1958

Ella is growing up and falls in love with Jules but war breaks out and Jules joins the Army.

Taylor, Sydney
5
Ella of All-of-a-Kind Family
Dutton, 1978

Jules returns from the war and wants to be alone with Ella. But how do you do that when there are six children in the family?

Taylor, Theodore
1
Teetoncey
Doubleday, 1974

Ben saves a shipwrecked girl on a stormy night and begins a suspenseful story. The girl will not speak and cannot remember anything about the accident.

Taylor, Theodore
2
Teetoncey and Ben O'Neal
Doubleday, 1975

An orphaned shipwrecked survivor, Teetoncey and Ben O'Neal, a fatherless boy, explore the rocky coast. Tee remembers a treasure being on the ship that sank and Ben tries to recover it.

Taylor, Theodore
3
Odyssey of Ben O'Neal
Doubleday, 1977

Ben grows up and accepts responsibility. He goes to Norfolk to look for his brother and Tee goes back to her home in England. But they unexpectedly meet again.

Thomas, Jane
1
Comeback Dog
Houghton, 1981

Daniel's dog dies and he feels he never wants another one. He finds an abandoned dog and cares for it. He calls it Lady. He is hurt when the dog does not immediately respond to his kindness.

Thomas, Jane
2
Fox in a Trap
Clarion, 1987

Daniel thinks trapping would be fun. But when he goes with Uncle Pete he finds that it has drawbacks. He faces a moral dilemma when he sees the cruelty involved.

Thomas, Joyce
1
Marked by Fire
Flare, 1982

Abby, a Black living in the South, learns the secrets of folk medicine from Mother Barker.

Thomas, Joyce
2
Bright Shadow

Flare, 1983

Abby finds that both love and education have their problems as well as their joys.

Thomas, Joyce
3
Out of the Shadow
Flare, 1983

Serious family problems and hard gained maturity makes life for Abby both difficult and easy.

Thrasher, Crystal
1
Dark Didn't Catch Me
Atheneum, 1975

The beginning of a story of a family that survives the Great Depression. Seely is the main character who lives through hard work, troubles, death and sorrows.

Thrasher, Crystal
2
Between Dark and Daylight
Atheneum, 1979

Seely, during the Depression, has her life changed by fire, death, threatened rape and murder.

Thrasher, Crystal
3
Julie's Summer
Atheneum, 1981

Julie is Seely's older sister, the one who remained behind when Seely moved. She has a couple of boyfriends but decides not to marry either one, and instead decides to go to college.

Thrasher, Crystal
4
End of a Dark Road
Atheneum, 1982

Seely's best friend, Russell, abused by his stepfather is "accidently" killed by him while hunting. Another friend is hurt in a hayride accident. Her father dies. But the future looks bright.

Thrasher, Crystal
5
Taste of Daylight
Atheneum, 1984

The last book in the series about Seely. It is still the time of the Great Depression but things are looking up for Seely. She moves out into the city in hopes of a better life.

Tolan, Stephanie
1
Great Skinner Strike
Macmillan, 1983

Jenny Skinner, 14, tells about her mother's strike. Home life is topsy-turvy for 19 days. Neighbors join in. Father and four children try to cope but can't. The two daughters join mother.

Tolan, Stephanie
2
Great Skinner Enterprise
Four Winds, 1986

Father has changed from conservative to flashy and is fired from his job. He starts a new service business at home and is so successful that it may ruin the family.

Tolan, Stephanie
3
Great Skinner Getaway
Four Winds, 1987

Father buys a motor home and they all set out for a cross-country trip to see everything and meet many people. Mother, Father, four children, two cats and one dog. It is disastrous.

Tolan, Stephanie
4
Great Skinner Homestead
Four Winds, 1988

The motor home breaks down in the Adirondacks. Father decides to homestead there. He and the family work for the land rent: weed picking and canning beans. Jenny meets a college boy and helps him.

Tolkien, J. R. R.
1
Hobbit
Houghton, 1937

The prelude to *Lord of the Rings*. The Hobbit is Bilbo Baggins and he lives in Middle Earth. His ring can make him disappear.

Tolkien, J. R. R.
2 (*Lord of the Rings* trilogy)
Fellowship of the Ring
Houghton, 1965
A young hobbit, Frodo, undertakes a journey to prevent a magic ring from falling into the hands of the powers of evil.

Tolkien, J. R. R.
3 (*Lord of the Rings* trilogy)
Two Towers
Houghton, 1965
This story tells how each member of the broken fellowship made out before the coming of the Great Darkness.

Tolkien, J. R. R.
4 (*Lord of the Rings* trilogy)
Return of the King
Houghton, 1965
Evil Dark Lord Sauron wants to conquer all Middle Earth. Gandalf, the wizard, with the help of Frodo, brings an end to the Great Darkness. The Ring must be destroyed.

Tolkien, J. R. R.
5
Silmarillion
Houghton, 1977
This book is background for *Lord of the Rings*. This and the *Hobbit* can be read separately, before or after and enjoyed as much as *Lord of the Rings*.

Tolles, Martha
1
Who's Reading Darci's Diary
Dutton, 1984
Darci had a secret diary. No one could see it. It included thoughts about her friends, her feelings and especially about Travis, a cute boy at school. Now it is missing. What should she do?

Tolles, Martha
2
Darci and the Dance Contest
Dutton, 1985
Darci moves from California to New York. She has not yet made friends. Nathan teases her. The girls ignore her. Should she enter the Dance Contest? If so, with whom? Nathan, of course.

Tomerlin, John
1
Magnificent Jalopy
Dutton, 1967
Wally, Link and Injun get an old '32 Packard and restore it. They take part in a rally on the West Coast. They rescue a man who is caught in an accident and take it in stride.

Tomerlin, John
2
Nothing Special
Dutton, 1969
Wally, Link and Injun build their own sports car to race. They must pass tests of Driver Training, get their car through Inspection and then race at Riverside. They must be a team.

Tomerlin, John
A1
Fledgling
Dutton, 1968
Rich meets the world of airplanes and flying. He wants to learn everything but his mother is against it. He is a little unsure of himself but friends build his confidence.

Tomerlin, John
A2
Sky Clowns
Dutton, 1973
Rich has learned a great deal about flying from Carlie Hatcher. He is now doing aerobatics himself. Is there a future for stunt fliers?

Touster, Irwin
1
Perez Arson Mystery
Dial, 1972
Antonio Perez was a nasty boy accused of arson when the store he was fired from burned down. Vernon, David and Penny investigate and prove him innocent.

Touster, Irwin
2
Runaway Bus Mystery
Dial, 1972
A school bus had an accident and Vernon is in the hospital. Was it brake

failure or careless driving? David and Penny investigate. A look at a real law case, our legal system and trial by jury.

Townsend, John
1
Trouble in the Jungle
Lippincott, 1961
The Jungle is a ghetto. The four Thompson children, Kevin, Sandra, Jean and Harold are left to fend for themselves and don't want a home when Father/Uncle returns with a mistress.

Townsend, John
2
Good-Bye to the Jungle
Lippincott, 1965
The Thompsons get to leave the Jungle for a new home in a housing development. This does not change their life and they still must struggle to make their way.

Townsend, John
3
Pirate's Island
Lippincott, 1968
When a real treasure is stolen from a trusting old man, Gordon and Sheila decide to help him find his treasure. Gordon was pursued by bullies and Sheila was his only friend.

Travers, Pamela
1
Mary Poppins
Harcourt, 1934
Magical Mary Poppins is an extraordinary lady, full of fun and excitement. The children knew she was magical right from the beginning.

Travers, Pamela
2
Mary Poppins Comes Back
Harcourt, 1935
More adventures with this delightful babysitter. She said she would return and she did. She arrived at the end of a kite string.

Travers, Pamela
3
Mary Poppins Opens the Door
Harcourt, 1943
Whimsical Mary is back with new adventures. This time she comes back on a falling spark and finds there is a new baby, Annabel.

Travers, Pamela
4
Mary Poppins in the Park
Harcourt, 1952
Mary Poppins brings Michael, Jane, the twins and Annabel the best in fun and enchanting adventures.

Travers, Pamela
5
Mary Poppins in the Cherry Tree
Delacorte, 1982
This book describes some of Mary's earlier adventures and is easier to read. It is more akin to Mary Poppins from A to Z and Mary Poppins in the kitchen.

Treece, Henry
1
Viking's Dawn
Criterion, 1956
Heroic saga of Vikings and their world in the eighth century. A voyage taken is one of hardship and death.

Treece, Henry
2
Road to Miklagard
Criterion, 1956
Harald and his fruitless trip to find treasure in what is now Ireland. He ends up in Spain where he is not wanted. He escapes back to his homeland. A story of cruelty and bravery.

Treece, Henry
3
Viking's Sunset
Criterion, 1960
The last battles of Harald. The story takes the reader out of Norway into Iceland, Greenland and North America.

Tunis, John R.
A1
Keystone Kids
Harcourt, 1943
Two brothers, Spike and Bob play

baseball. One plays second base and the other, shortstop. Their team is poorly managed. Spike becomes manager but has a lot of work to do to make a team.

Tunis, John R.
A2
Rookie of the Year
Harcourt, 1944
  A young rookie pitcher, because of the coach's faith in him, takes his team from fourth to first place.

Tunis, John R.
A3
Kid Comes Back
Morrow, 1946
  After fighting in France and Germany Roy comes back to play baseball again. He again saves the game for his teammates.

Tunis, John R.
B1
Iron Duke
Harcourt, 1938
  Mickey is in college and makes the adjustment well. His grades are good and he makes the track team. He is a great runner.

Tunis, John R.
B2
Duke Decides
Harcourt, 1939
  The Duke is a determined athlete who trains hard to win. He makes the Olympic team and is the fastest man alive.

Turner, Phillip
1
Colonel Sheperton's Clock
World, 1964
  Peter, David and Arthur stumble on a mystery. They find a clue in an old 1914 newspaper that leads to Colonel Sheperton, a World War I hero and his grandfather clock. There they find a secret.

Turner, Phillip
2
Grange at High Force

World, 1967
  This time Peter, David and Arthur hunt for a lost statue that has been missing for centuries. A humorous adventure helped by a retired admiral.

Turner, Phillip
3
Sea Peril
World, 1966
  Peter, David and Arthur plan, construct and operate a bicycle-powered punt in which they plan to explore the river. The boys find both friends and enemies in their quest.

Turner, Phillip
4
War on the Darnel
World, 1969
  Peter, David and Arthur fight with another set of boys who have set up a barricade on the river and are charging a fee. It is all in the name of a charity and ends up funny and clever.

Uchida, Yoshika
1
Journey to Topaz
Scribner, 1971
  The story of a Japanese family in California at the outbreak of World War II and their experiences in interment camps. Yuki and Ken's father are separated from them.

Uchida, Yoshika
2
Journey Home
Atheneum, 1978
  Even though they are released from camp at war's end, the family has difficulty getting resettled. Ken returns from the war wounded and emotionally unstable.

Uchida, Yoshika
A1
Jar of Dreams
Atheneum, 1981
  Rinko grew up in Oakland, California, during the Great Depression. Her Aunt Waka from Japan comes to visit and although she sees the prejudices she inspires the whole family.

Uchida, Yoshika
A2
Best Bad Thing
Atheneum, 1983

Riiiko must spend the summer with Mrs. Hata and her two sons. She has her own ideas about this help for a lady she is sure she will not like. One disaster follows another.

Ure, Jean
1
See You Thursday
Delacorte, 1981

Sixteen-year-old Marianne attends a girls' school. She finds a friend in Abe, a piano teacher who has been blind since birth.

Ure, Jean
2
After Thursday
Delacorte, 1985

Marianne is in love with Abe but he wants to pursue his career. Peter enters her life but she still is devoted to Abe. There will be more complications before this is settled.

Van Leeuwen, Jean
1
Great Cheese Conspiracy
Random, 1969

A gang of mice, Marvin, Fats and Raymond invade the nearest cheese store. They have narrow escapes, Fats trips the alarm and they are caught. It comes out alright even though Marvin doesn't like it.

Van Leeuwen, Jean
2
Great Christmas Kidnapping
Dial, 1975

Macy's Santa Claus has been kidnapped by Gimbel's Santa Claus. Marvin, Fats and Raymond send a letter using words clipped from a newspaper to the police giving them leads and Santa is rescued.

Van Leeuwen, Jean
3
Great Rescue Operation
Dial, 1982

Marvin and Raymond have lost Fats to a person who bought a doll carriage with him in it. They dream up fantastic schemes for his rescue.

Van Leeuwen, Jean
A1
Benjy and the Power of Zingies
Dial, 1982

Benjy doesn't want to be the town's weakling, the one everyone picks on. He sees an ad for a breakfast cereal that will build your body and he goes for it.

Van Leeuwen, Jean
A2
Benjy in Business
Dial, 1983

Benjy needs money for a fielder's mill, to improve his game. He goes into several businesses: lemonade, car and/ or dog wash, selling old toys, pulling weeds, etc.

Van Leeuwen, Jean
A3
Benjy, the Football Hero
Dial, 1985

Benjy plays great football. He is the class star. But a challenge is coming. Alex and his boys against Benjy, Case the Ace and Killer Kelly (a girl).

Verney, John
1
Friday's Tunnel
Holt, 1960

February and Friday are sister and brother. When their father disappears while traveling to Capria for a rare mineral, Caprium, they get involved. Friday's tunnel becomes a hiding place.

Verney, John
2
February's Road
Holt, 1961

Feb and Mike, a journalist, try to find out what is behind the strange happenings on the road through Marsh Manor.

Verney, John
3
Ismo
Holt, 1964

There is a wide-reaching plot to steal some art treasures by an international organization. The story is complete with secret agents and passwords.

Vipont, Elfrida
1
Lark in the Morn
Holt, 1951
Kit has a talent for singing. She enters a school where they discover this talent. Her family, being Quakers, are not in favor of her singing.

Vipont, Elfrida
2
Lark on the Wing
Holt, 1950
Kit studies music despite family resistence. She reaches her goal with the help of Papa Andrean and Terry.

Vogel, Ilse-Marget
1
Dodo Every Day
Harper, 1977
Dodo is the ideal grandmother by being amusing and loving every time she is needed.

Vogel, Ilse-Marget
2
Farewell, Aunt Isabell
Harper, 1979
Inge and Erika try to cheer up Aunt Isabell so she can get well. She is going to take them to Paris when she feels better, but they don't understand her illness.

Vogel, Ilse-Marget
3
My Twin Sister Erika
Harper, 1976
Inge and Erika have a rocky relationship. One day she said in anger that she wishes Erika dead; later Erika died of a disease and Inge feels guilty and misses her in spite of her jealousy.

Vogel, Ilse-Marget
4
My Summer Brother
Harper, 1981
Erika is away, Dodo, her grandmother is gone also. She meets Dieter, a 20-year-old, and likes him right away. But so does her mother. She finds her "first love" is not a good one.

Vogel, Ilse-Marget
5
Tikhon
Harper, 1984
Inge meets Tikhon, a Russian soldier, and a deep friendship begins between a soldier who is lonely away from home and a little girl. They have common interests and Inge thinks Tikhon can do anything.

Voigt, Cynthia
1
Homecoming
Atheneum, 1981
Abandoned by their mother, four children begin a search for home, possibly with a great-aunt or maybe grandparents. Dicey holds the three children, Sammy, James and Maybeth together.

Voigt, Cynthia
2
Dicey's Song
Atheneum, 1982
The four children find a home with their grandmother and Dicey must decide what she wants for herself and her brothers and sisters.

Voigt, Cynthia
3
Solitary Blue
Atheneum, 1983
Jeff is torn between love for a deserted mother and a professor father. He gets to know them both better and decides. He meets Dicey in high school where they are both new students.

Voigt, Cynthia
4
Come a Stranger
Atheneum, 1986
Mina, a Black dancer, defended Dicey when she was accused of plagerism in an earlier book and Tamer, a Black friend from another book, who is now a minister, get together when Mina needs help.

Wahl, Jan
1
Furious Flycycle
Delacorte, 1968
Melvin discovers what makes baseballs fly and uses this information to build a flying machine with his bicycle. He rescues relatives from hungry wolves.

Wahl, Jan
2
S.O.S. Bobomobile
Delacorte, 1973
Marvin and his professor friend go underseas with their new invention: the bobomobile. They look for the Loch Ness monster.

Walker, Diana
1
Year of the Horse
Abelard, 1975
Joanna wants to learn to ride. She also wants to meet John Holmes. But her horse, Horse, is not as regal and impressive as John's. She has a fabulous year anyway.

Walker, Diana
2
Mother Wants a Horse
Abelard, 1978
Joanna must give up some of her horse time to studies. She runs away on a "borrowed" horse and is seriously hurt. She is forced to study and when she recovers sees life from a different angle.

Wallace, Barbara
1
Hello, Claudia
Follett, 1982
Claudia and Janice are best friends when Janice moves away. She finds a friend in Duffy even though he is younger and a boy.

Wallace, Barbara
2
Claudia and Duffy
Follett, 1982
Claudia has many friends but Duffy has only Claudia. This causes problems for Claudia.

Wallace, Barbara
3
Claudia
Follett, 1969
Claudia and Duffy are still friends when her old friend Janis moves back. But she is not the same and the friendship is strained. Her parents want her to be friends with Janis not Duffy.

Wallace, Barbara
A1
Hawkins
Smith, 1977
Hawkins, a gentleman's gentleman, seems to be around when needed. Harvey gets into one scrape after another but Hawkins is there to rescue him.

Wallace, Barbara
A2
Contest Kid Strikes Again
Abingdon, 1980
Harvey loves anything that's free—12 chickens! 575 marbles! His wild escapades and funny dilemmas don't always work out. But Hawkins is always there to help when needed.

Wallace, Barbara
A3
Hawkins and the Soccer Solution
Abingdon, 1981
Harvey and his friends raise money to solve the problem of their losing soccer team. Hawkins, "a gentleman's gentleman," helps by becoming coach.

Wallace, Barbara
B1
Trouble with Miss Switch
Archway, 1981
Miss Switch is the fifth grade teacher. Because of her unusual ways and because it is such a natural for the kids, she is named Miss Switch, the witch.

Wallace, Barbara
B2
Miss Switch to the Rescue
Abingdon, 1981
Rupert's friend Amelia is kidnapped. Miss Switch, the witch of the fifth grade, comes along just in time.

Walsh, Jill P.
1
Goldengrove
Farrar, 1972
Madge finds out that her feelings for her cousin Paul are changing. She finds friendship with a blind professor for whom she reads.

Walsh, Jill P.
2
Unleaving
Farrar; 1976
Madge inherits Goldengrove from her grandmother and decides to rent it. Madge meets Patrick and falls in love.

Webb, Sharon
1
Earthchild
Atheneum, 1982
When the Earth becomes immortal, through the Mouai Gari process, a young musician realizes he may live forever but his creativity is going to gradually fade away. This can't be.

Webb, Sharon
2
Earth Song
Atheneum, 1983
Earth Song can achieve immortality, but creativity is crushed. This is a high price to pay. Creativity must be restored.

Webb, Sharon
3
Ram Song
Atheneum, 1984
A strange beam on the planet Aulos disorients people in interrupting a yearly festival. Kurt Kraus, now immortal, and his starship, Ram, are called to help.

Weber, Lenora
1
Meet the Malones
Crowell, 1943
The Malone family is father Martie, brother Johnny, 15, Mary, 16 and Beany, 13. Beany will be the main character in this series but she interacts with the whole family.

Weber, Lenora
2
Beany Malone
Crowell, 1948
Beany is a sophomore in high school. She is not the beauty queen or of that set; she is not an intellect or of that set, either. But she is known as a doer to her family and friends.

Weber, Lenora
3
Leave It to Beany
Crowell, 1950
Beany gives advice to the lovelorn through a newspaper column and makes the necessary adjustments to her family and Sheila. She helps people and gets into unpredictable situations.

Weber, Lenora
4
Beany and the Beckoning Road
Crowell, 1952
Beany and her brother Johnny travel to California. She is unhappy with her boyfriend, Norbett, and wants a change. They are short of money and have a strange, "motherly" nonpaying guest.

Weber, Lenora
5
Beany Has a Secret Life
Crowell, 1955
Beany joins a secret club but it separates her from her family especially her stepmother. Norbett is not coming back from Ohio and she finds a new friend in Andy.

Weber, Lenora
6
Make a Wish for Me
Crowell, 1956
Beany renews the friendship of her old boyfriend, Norbett, and starts a new friendship with a new girl in school, Dulcie, but she flirts with Norbett even though Beany is wearing his bracelet.

Weber, Lenora
7
Happy Birthday Dear Beany
Crowell, 1957
Beany is now 17. Norbett is still very

much in her life. Her old friend Miggs is acting strange and Beany starts seeing Hank a lot instead of Norbett.

Weber, Lenora

8

More the Merrier

Crowell, 1958

Beany Malone takes in boarders during the summer her family is away. She wants to make some money but she gives shy Lisa a reduced rate out of pity and Ty a free ride because she likes him.

Weber, Lenora

9

Bright Star Falls

Crowell, 1959

Beany's brother, Johnny, has a new girlfriend who is the talk of the town. Beany is a sophomore and the editor of the school paper. Andy comes home from the Marines but is bitter and hurt.

Weber, Lenora

10

Welcome, Stranger

Crowell, 1960

Andy takes Beany out while home on leave. She turns to Tony when she feels deserted by her family and misunderstood by Andy and her friends. She and Tony have in common a guilt about an accident.

Weber, Lenora

11

Pick a New Dream

Crowell, 1961

Beany graduates from high school and doesn't get the summer job she was promised. Andy is not sympathetic because he has problems of his own. She finds solace in Carlton from next door.

Weber, Lenora

12

Tarry Awhile

Crowell, 1962

Beany realizes that it is Carlton that she truly loves. She is engaged and wants to marry as all her friends are doing. But Carlton wants to wait until he graduates before getting married.

Weber, Lenora

13

Something Borrowed, Something Blue

Crowell, 1963

Beany and Carlton are to be married. This is the story about how this warm, tight-knit family is involved in this happy event. It could turn out to be very posh but returns to be very simple.

Weber, Lenora

14

Come Back, Wherever You Are

Crowell, 1969

Beany Malone is married and takes in the orphaned son of an old friend. She and Carlton have two children of their own and Jodey is a disturbed child who threatens her own family.

Weber, Lenora

A1

Don't Call Me Katie Rose

Crowell, 1964

Katie Rose wants to be called Kathleen. She is Stacy's older sister. Her mother plays piano in a night club for extra money. Katie Rose is embarrassed by this.

Weber, Lenora

A2

Winds of March

Crowell, 1965

Katie Rose is over her crush on Bruce. His failing grades prompts her to tutor him. Her crush is renewed. But it's Stacy, her sister, that he likes. She doesn't get a role in the school play!

Weber, Lenora

A3

New and Different Summer

Crowell, 1966

Katie Rose is left in charge of all five of the other children. She disregards her mother's "from scratch" cooking and buys from the frozen food section of the supermarket.

Weber, Lenora

A4

I Met a Boy I Used to Know

Crowell, 1967

Katie Rose is a junior. She meets Gil

who has transferred to her school from California. Although he is an only child and Katie Rose has brothers and sisters they both have mother problems.

Weber, Lenora
A5
Angel in Heavy Shoes
Crowell, 1968

Katie Rose enters a playwriting contest. But her family activities always interferes with her work, especially Stacy and her boyfriend Bruce. She appears to have nothing but problems.

Weber, Lenora
B1
How Long Is Always?
Crowell, 1970

Stacy gets a summer job driving her employer around his ranch. She is courted by two boys from the community and finds herself involved deeper in the community than she wanted to be.

Weber, Lenora
B2
Hello, My Love, Goodbye
Crowell, 1971

Stacy is a senior at high school and has lots of friends, especially one boy named Bruce. He is from a background very different from Stacy's.

Weber, Lenora
B3
Sometimes a Stranger
Crowell, 1972

Bruce's parents don't like Stacy. They offered Bruce a new car if he would stop seeing her. Stacy is furious but a separation changes Bruce and Stacy sees other boys.

Wersba, Barbara
1
Fat, a Love Story
Harper, 1987

Rita, an overweight 16-year-old, meets Robert, a school athlete and falls "in love." She tries to lose weight but she works in a bakery with Arnold and it is a struggle.

Wersba, Barbara
2
Love Is the Crooked Thing
Harper, 1987

Rita, now 17 and still fat, writes a "hot romance" to make some money. She wants to find her old friend Arnold.

Wersba, Barbara
3
Beautiful Losers
Harper, 1988

Now Rita is 18 and although she is still fat she has become a successful writer. She finds Arnold and their love affair begins but it is not without problems.

Westall, Robert
1
Machine Gunners
Greenwillow, 1976

Charles McGill finds a machine gun on a shot-down pilot near his home. He and his friend plan to use it against the Germans. They capture a German pilot who fixes the machine gun.

Westall, Robert
2
Fathom Five
Greenwillow, 1979

Charles spends the Spring of 1943 trying to discover who the spy in Garmouth is and why he is passing information to the Germans. Then he faces the problem of what to do about it.

Westall, Robert
3
Haunting of Charles McGill
Greenwillow, 1983

Charles McGill finds a ghost in an old abandoned house. The ghost turns out to be a World War I deserter.

Wibberley, Leonard
1
Mouse That Roared
Little, 1955

This is a story about a tiny European principality, Grand Fenwick, located in the Swiss Alps. It is governed by a Duchy and is three miles by five miles in size. It declares war on the United States.

Wibberley, Leonard
2
Mouse on the Moon
Morrow, 1962
Lilliput heads for the moon in a junked United States rocket. By getting there before the United States or Russia it can save the moon.

Wibberley, Leonard
3
Mouse on Wall Street
Morrow, 1969
By burning all the paper money in the United States, Grand Fenwick saves the world from economic disaster.

Wibberley, Leonard
4
Mouse That Saved the West
Morrow, 1981
Grand Fenwick defeats the OPEC nations and thereby solves the world's oil problems.

Wibberley, Leonard
A1
Leopard's Prey
Farrar, 1971
Prior to the War of 1812 Treegate is chased by pirates and is rescued by a Haitian witch.

Wibberley, Leonard
A2
Red Pawn
Farrar, 1973
A story of the Battle of Tippecanoe under Tecumseh. Manly and Peter Treegate find themselves aboard the same ship.

Wibberley, Leonard
A3
Last Battle
Farrar, 1976
This is the story of a Naval battle during the War of 1812, outside of New Orleans. Pete is injured. Manly comes home with captured enemy papers.

Wibberley, Leonard
B1
John Treegate's Musket
Farrar, 1959

Peter, John Treegate's son, gets involved in a dock murder and flees arrest during the Revolutionary War. John was a loyalist but followed Peter's allegiance to the Colonies.

Wibberley, Leonard
B2
Peter Treegate's War
Farrar, 1960
Peter has conflicting loyalties during the Revolutionary War. He is captured but escapes on a prison barge manned by fisherman, Peace of God Manly.

Wibberley, Leonard
B3
Sea Captain from Salem
Farrar, 1961
The Revolutionary War moves to the French shipping lanes where Captain Peace of God Manly sabotages English ships with his one boat.

Wibberley, Leonard
B4
Treegate's Raiders
Farrar, 1962
Two significant battles at the climax of the Revolutionary War and the surrender at Yorktown.

Wibberley, Leonard
C1
Black Tiger
Washburn, 1956
This book is about Woody Hartford who displayed courage when he raced the powerful Black Tiger after two mysterious accidents.

Wibberley, Leonard
C2
Mexican Road Race
Washburn, 1957
Black Tiger, a race car runs a grueling 2,000 mile race with twisting turns and a few accidents.

Wibberley, Leonard
C3
Black Tiger at Le Mans
Washburn, 1958
This time the race is in exciting Le Mans. Woody and his partner, Worm

McNess compete in the Black Tiger Mark II against their rival Von Ritwir.

Wibberley, Leonard
C4
Black Tiger at Indianapolis
Washburn, 1962

Woody Hartford and his racing car, Black Tiger, along with Worm, stake out the track at Indianapolis' great 500.

Wibberley, Leonard
C5
Black Tiger at Bonneville
Washburn, 1960

Woody and his partner, Worm, challenge the land speed record at Bonneville in the Black Tiger against Von Ritwir.

Wibberley, Leonard
C6
Car Called Camellia
Washburn, 1970

When the Black Tiger company won't sponsor the car, Worm McNess builds a new one with a steam turbine.

Wilder, Cherry
1
Princess of the Chameln
Atheneum, 1984

Firn, now an orphan, flees to gather strength to free her people.

Wilder, Cherry
2
Yorath, the Wolf
Atheneum, 1984

Reared in secret because of a birth defect, Yorath, prince and heir to the throne of Mel Nir, learns of his heritage after some strange adventures. He must decide what he is to do now.

Wilder, Cherry
A1
Luck of Brin's Five
Atheneum, 1977

The planet Torin is visited by inhabitants of the Earth and their social order, run by strict standards, is altered.

Wilder, Cherry
A2
Nearest Fire
Atheneum, 1980

Four Earthmen, one separated from the rest, elude being captured by the Great Elder on the planet, Torin.

Wilder, Cherry
A3
Tapestry Warriors
Atheneum, 1983

The four Earthmen, reunited, live quietly on the planet, Torin, until a diviner tries to seize power.

Wilder, Laura
1
Little House in the Big Woods
Harper, 1932

Laura and her family live in the unsettled West. This book is about their first year of trying to survive. The family is Ma, Pa, Mary, Carrie and, of course, Laura.

Wilder, Laura
2
Little House on the Prairie
Harper, 1935

Laura moves West to Kansas and discovers both beauty and fear. One night wolves surround the whole house. Laura and Mary have many chores and lead busy lives.

Wilder, Laura
3
Farmer Boy
Harper, 1933

This is the story of Almanzo Wilder, the farmer boy Laura will one day marry. He lives on a farm in New York with his sisters and brother. They, too, are busy performing farm chores.

Wilder, Laura
4
On the Banks of Plum Creek
Harper, 1937

Laura, with her parents, move to a new house on Plum Creek. But tragedy strikes in the form of grasshoppers.

Wilder, Laura
5
By the Shores of Silver Lake
Harper, 1939

This book describes a railroad building camp, where Laura's father now works. He finds a home site and sends for his family.

Wilder, Laura
6
Long Winter
Harper, 1940
Because he suspects a hard winter, Mr. Ingalls moves his family into town. But because blizzards cut off the town from supplies Pa must cross the prairie to get wheat.

Wilder, Laura
7
Little Town on the Prairie
Harper, 1941
This book describes life as it was lived in the Dakota Territory. Laura goes to a social and meets Almanzo. She also gets her certificate to teach school.

Wilder, Laura
8
These Happy, Golden Days
Harper, 1943
Laura, not yet 16, becomes a school teacher and when her term is over she marries Almanzo Wilder.

Wilder, Laura
9
First Four Years
Harper, 1971
Laura and Almanzo settle in South Dakota to spend their first years together. Their daughter Rose is born.

Wilkinson, Brenda
1
Ludell
Harper, 1975
Ludell, a Black girl, has both the pleasures and the pains of growing up in the '50s. Her best friend is Ruthie Mae who lives next door. Her brother, Willie, also becomes friends with Ludell.

Wilkinson, Brenda
2
Ludell and Willie
Harper, 1977
Ludell and Willie become better

friends and want to spend more time together but Ludell's grandmother is very strict and causes tension. When Grandmother gets ill Ludell nurses her.

Wilkinson, Brenda
3
Ludell's New York Time
Harper, 1980
Ludell's grandmother dies and Ludell moves to Harlem, leaving Willie and her plans of a wedding. Willie is busy with family problems in Georgia and Ludell has problems in New York.

Willard, Barbara
1
Lark and the Laurel
Harcourt, 1970
Cecily, 16, goes to live with her aunt where she is educated and meets a neighbor, Lewis. She doesn't want to return to live with her strict father. She loves Mantlemass Manor.

Willard, Barbara
2
Sprig of Broom
Dutton, 1971
A tale of what might have happened to the last sprig of the Plantagenet family tree in Tudor England. When Medley marries into Mantlemass Manor he learns its significance.

Willard, Barbara
3
Cold Wind Blowing
Dutton, 1972
The young Englishman Piers Medley, finds himself the guardian to a mysterious, silent girl. This girl's true identity effects everyone in the Medley family.

Willard, Barbara
4
Iron Lily
Dutton, 1973
Lilas is left an orphan by the plague and tries to find some link with her family. She has a crest ring and her baptism paper with the name Medley.

Willard, Barbara
5

Harrow and Harvest
Dutton, 1974

The Medley family and their ancestral home, Mantlemass, are drawn into the conflict of the English Civil War. This scatters the family more than the records Cecilia inherits from her grandmother.

Willard, Nancy
1
Sailing to Cythera
Harcourt, 1985

Anatole tells three stories: To cross the river he exchanges his shirt and shoes for a raft; with the help of two ravens he aids a soldier with his memory; he befriends Blimlim, a monster.

Willard, Nancy
2
Island of the Grass King
Harcourt, 1979

Anatole needs to find a cure for his grandmother's asthma. He finds a winged horse and is ready to go where the herb he needs grows. He, his cat, Plumpet (and a coffeepot) go on the journey.

Willard, Nancy
3
Uncle Terrible
Harcourt, 1982

Uncle Terrible is really terribly nice. He and Anatole have wonderful adventures. When Uncle Terrible is turned into a snake only Anatole can help him. He must win a bizarre checker game.

Williams, Barbara
1
Mitzi and the Terrible Tyrannasaurus
Dutton, 1982

Mitzi's mother is about to marry Walter (and his boys). Mitzi doesn't like it. Who could think that Darwin and Frederick could be so interesting?

Williams, Barbara
2
Mitzi's Honeymoon with Nana Potts
Dutton, 1983

Mitzi's mother is on her honeymoon. She is stuck with Darwin and Frederick. And Nana Potts who didn't act like a grandmother should. Darwin was completely obnoxious.

Williams, Barbara
3
Mitzi and Frederick the Great
Dutton, 1984

Mitzi is going on an archeological dig and loves it. But bossy Frederick is going, too. He reads books and is liked by grown-ups. But he turns out to be not too bad and the Indian ruins were great.

Williams, Barbara
4
Mitzi and the Elephants
Dutton, 1985

Mitzi wants a pet. She is offered a free St. Bernard puppy. But her parents think she is not responsible enough. She helps a man in the zoo who keeps elephants and proves herself. She gets her dog.

Williams, Jay
1
Danny Dunn and the Antigravity Paint
McGraw-Hill, 1956

Professor Bullfinch hangs from the ceiling after stepping in the antigravity paint. He and Danny go into outer space.

Williams, Jay
2
Danny Dunn on a Desert Island
McGraw-Hill, 1957

Joe, Danny and Professor Bullfinch are stranded in the desert after their plane crashed.

Williams, Jay
3
Danny Dunn
and the Homework Machine
McGraw-Hill, 1958

What happens when Danny decides to let MANIAC do his homework and someone sabotages the machine?

Williams, Jay
4
Danny Dunn
and the Weather-Making Machine
McGraw-Hill, 1959

Danny, Irene and Joe can create thunderstorms. This leads to hilarious adventures.

Williams, Jay
5
Danny Dunn on the Ocean Floor
McGraw-Hill, 1960
Another of Danny's scientifically possible adventures in a bathyscaphe. An accident happens and they go deeper than planned. But it leads to an Aztec treasure.

Williams, Jay
6
Danny Dunn and the Fossil Cave
McGraw-Hill, 1961
Danny stumbles onto a cave and another adventure begins.

Williams, Jay
7
Danny Dunn and the Heat Ray
McGraw-Hill, 1962
Danny uses up-to-the-minute scientific data; he uses the LASER for practical application with humorous results.

Williams, Jay
8
Danny Dunn, Time Traveler
McGraw-Hill, 1963
This time Danny has a time machine to lead him on his funny, believable adventure.

Williams, Jay
9
Danny Dunn and the Automated House
McGraw-Hill, 1965
Danny and Professor Bullfinch design a house full of robots for Danny's science fair project. Danny gets trapped in the house and all the mechanisms go haywire.

Williams, Jay
10
Danny Dunn and the Voice from Space
McGraw-Hill, 1967
In this story Danny goes to England. He and his friends have their usual equipment and they use a radio telescope to see if they can communicate with someone on another planet.

Williams, Jay
11
Danny Dunn and the Smallifying Machine
McGraw-Hill, 1969
Danny tries a lever and he, his friend and a dog are trapped in the machine. He is shrinking fast! He is down to the size of a thimble. Luckily someone sees this and pulls the proper switches.

Williams, Jay
12
Danny Dunn and the Swamp Monster
Hall, 1973
Danny searches for the legendary serpent in Central Africa. Lots of adventure along the shores of the Nile. It turns out to be a giant electric catfish.

Williams, Jay
13
Danny Dunn, Invisible Boy
McGraw-Hill, 1974
Danny put out a fire with some liquid in the Professor's lab. It melted rare crystals and the invisible machine was invented. But government officials want to confiscate it.

Williams, Jay
14
Danny Dunn, Scientific Detective
McGraw-Hill, 1975
Danny and his friends set out to clear Professor Bullfinch of suspicion and find a thief. They find the missing department store manager with a bloodhound robot.

Williams, Jay
15
Danny Dunn and the Universal Glue
McGraw-Hill, 1977
Danny goes fishing with his new invention and ends up saving a dam. A new pollutant is harmless to humans but destroys concrete.

Wilson, Hazel
1

Herbert
Knopf, 1950

Herbert is a boy with big ideas and his parents give him free rein. He collects, builds, changes, etc., and only Uncle Horace saves him from disaster time after time.

Wilson, Hazel
2

Herbert Again
Knopf, 1951

Herbert is always into something, mostly trouble. He has a gumdrop tree and x-ray glasses; he gives a horse a permanent wave and tames a bluejay with cereal and milk.

Wilson, Hazel
3

More Fun with Herbert
Knopf, 1954

This time Herbert has a pet mouse, Ambrose, who can sing! He uses his teeth braces as a radio receiver.

Wilson, Hazel
4

Herbert's Homework
Knopf, 1960

A mechanical brain helps Herbert with his homework. He spends more time getting the material ready to feed into the machine than if he did it himself.

Wilson, Hazel
5

Herbert's Space Trip
Knopf, 1965

Herbert, the innovative inventor, has really got into something this time. Even Uncle Horace may be of no help. But Herbert is undaunted.

Wilson, Hazel
6

Herbert's Stilts
Knopf, 1972

Herbert has carved animals on his stilts. He has all sorts of interaction with these same real animals: his dog, a kangaroo, etc.

Winterfield, Henry
1

Detective in Togas
Harcourt, 1956

This story focuses on Caius, whose father is a senator, and Rufus, whose father is a general and five others, who try to become detectives when Rufus is wrongly accused of graffiti.

Winterfield, Henry
2

Mystery of the Roman Ransom
Harcourt, 1969

The purchase of a slave, a Gaul with a secret message, for their teacher, leads these Roman students into danger and an assassination plot of their fathers.

Winthrop, Elizabeth
1

Marathon, Miranda
Holiday, 1979

Miranda meets Phoebe while walking her dog, Frisbee, in the park; her summer looks bright. She learns to jog in spite of asthma. Phoebe learns she is adopted and Miranda helps her accept this.

Winthrop, Elizabeth
2

Miranda in the Middle
Holiday, 1980

Miranda is losing both of her friends, one because she is marrying her grandfather; Phoebe because she finds a boyfriend. Miranda needs to find herself and evaluate her friends.

Wisler, G. C.
1

Buffalo Moon
Lodestar, 1984

Fourteen-year-old Willie leaves a Texas ranch and stays with Comanche Indians. He learns a great deal about life and its hazards.

Wisler, G. C.
2

Thunder on the Tennessee
Lodestar, 1983

Willie joins the Second Texas Regiment and leaves Texas to fight for the Confederacy. He is wounded during the Battle of Shiloh.

Woolley, Catherine
1
Ginnie and Geneva
Morrow, 1948
Ginnie was tutored at home and goes to school for the first time years after everyone else. She knows no one but meets Geneva, the class leader and Anna, an orphan and likes school a lot.

Woolley, Catherine
2
Ginnie Joins In
Morrow, 1951
Ginnie spends the summer at the lake but she is so unsure of herself she feels badly. She is envious of Joan because of her good looks, of Geneva because of her sense of humor. What about her?

Woolley, Catherine
3
Ginnie and the New Girl
Morrow, 1954
Ginnie and Geneva are best friends until Marcia comes along. She and Geneva are friendly and Ginnie is hurt but she soon comes to terms with the situation.

Woolley, Catherine
4
Ginnie and the Mystery House
Morrow, 1957
Ginnie and Geneva are collecting for a rummage sale. They found an old house with strange sounds. They befriend an old spinster and her dog. Their friend Peter helps.

Woolley, Catherine
5
Ginnie and the Mystery Doll
Morrow, 1960
Ginnie is on Cape Cod where she learns about an antique doll with a valuable necklace that is missing. Ginnie and Geneva find the doll and the jewel.

Woolley, Catherine
6
Ginnie and Her Juniors
Morrow, 1963
Ginnie wants to earn money for Christmas. She organized a babysitting service in her home.

Woolley, Catherine
7
Ginnie and the Cooking Contest
Morrow, 1966
Ginnie wants to win a trip to Washington, D.C. She finds recipes and cooks for her family and friends. She doesn't win but does get satisfaction from her help in the swimming pool project.

Woolley, Catherine
8
Ginnie and the Wedding Bells
Morrow, 1967
Ginnie is asked to be bridesmaid but a series of events almost prevent it: a black eye by a thrown snowball, a case of flu, bad weather, a cat's missing kittens. She does participate.

Woolley, Catherine
9
Ginnie and the Mystery Cat
Morrow, 1969
The ever sleuthing Ginnie, who loves a mystery, finds one involving a cat that has a surprising solution.

Woolley, Catherine
10
Ginnie and the Mystery Light
Morrow, 1973
Ginnie spends Christmas holidays in South Carolina where she sees a strange light that the local people think is a ghost or black magic. She solves the mystery and stops some superstitions.

Woolley, Catherine
A1
Room for Cathy
Morrow, 1956
Cathy wants a room of her own. Her family moves to a larger house and she gets one. But because of finances they must take in boarders and she loses her room again.

Woolley, Catherine
A2
Miss Cathy Leonard

Morrow, 1958

Cathy wants the town library to be in her house during summer vacation. She also has a friend coming to town for whom she must find a place to live.

Woolley, Catherine
A3
Cathy Leonard Calling
Morrow, 1961

Cathy is working as a social reporter on the County Crier and succeeds in both her school work and her "career."

Woolley, Catherine
A4
Cathy's Little Sister
Morrow, 1964

Chris is Cathy's younger sister. She wants to follow Cathy everywhere and be part of everything. She meets a friend whose three-year-old sister wants to do the same thing and doesn't like it.

Woolley, Catherine
A5
Chris in Trouble
Morrow, 1968

While Cathy and her mother were away, Chris and her visitor, Mary Ellen, sneaks into school. Chris goes back to get a doll left behind. Trouble again.

Woolley, Catherine
A6
Cathy and the Beautiful People
Morrow, 1971

A rock festival is coming to town. Cathy finds the people strange and different but she is attracted to them. Her parents are against the group but the generation gap is closed by common agreement.

Woolley, Catherine
A7
Cathy Uncovers a Secret
Morrow, 1972

Cathy does a lot of research before she uncovers the secret of the old house built during the Civil War. An old lady gives a clue as does a found black feather in the writing desk: A Lincoln letter.

Woolley, Catherine
B1

Look Alive, Libby
Morrow, 1962

Libby, 12, lives in New York in an apartment. She goes to spend the summer at Cape Cod. She finds that she can be quite independent.

Woolley, Catherine
B2
Libby Looks for a Spy
Morrow, 1965

Libby spends the winter at Cape Cod. She plays a big role in locating a spy when she hears neighbors talking about it. The discovery surprises even her.

Woolley, Catherine
B3
Libby's Uninvited Guest
Morrow, 1970

Libby spends the Christmas holidays on Cape Cod. Her serene vacation is interrupted when a strange intruder starts her investigating yet another mystery.

Woolley, Catherine
B4
Libby Shadows a Lady
Morrow, 1974

Libby spends Easter vacation in New York City. She overheard telephone conversation about a bombing. When she saw the caller again she followed her. All her efforts ended in stopping a crime.

Wrightson, Patricia
1
Nargon and the Stars
Atheneum, 1974

Simon Brent is the first one to have ever seen the monster. It is almost indistinguishable from Earth as it moves toward his home. He and his cousins must find a way to divert it.

Wrightson, Patricia
2
Ice Is Coming
Atheneum, 1977

A story of adventure, danger and high deeds. Ruthless ancient forces of fire and ice fight an epic struggle with the oldest Nargun and his people.

Wrightson, Patricia
3
Dark Bright Water
Atheneum, 1978
Wirrun, the hero, an Australian aborigine, helps save his "people," with the help of Mimi, when strange events occur on their continent.

Wrightson, Patricia
4
Journey Behind the Wind
Atheneum, 1981
Wirrun is called upon to free his land from red-eyed things. They are menacing visages who have no bodies and steal men's spirits.

Yolen, Jane
1
Dragon's Blood
Delacorte, 1982
Jakkin trains dragons in hopes of winning his freedom. He works as a keeper in a dragon nursery on the planet Austar IV. He communicates with the dragon telepathically.

Yolen, Jane
2
Heart's Blood

Delacorte, 1984
Jakkin is now free and has adventures with his favorite pit dragon, Heart's Blood.

Yolen, Jane
3
Sending of Dragons
Delacorte, 1987
Jakkin and Akki are accused of sabotage and are sent to another planet. They survive and gain both power and insight.

Zindel, Paul
1
Pigman
Harper, 1968
John Conlan and Lorraine Jensen are introduced to a lonely old man, Mr. Pignati, who befriends them. They betray that trust and Mr. Pignati dies.

Zindel, Paul
2
Pigman Legacy
Harper, 1980
Another adventure of John Lorraine with an old man. They feel badly about Mr. Pignati and want to atone for it.

Index

C

D

K

L

T

W

Y

Z